The Core Teachings

佛法要義

Other Works by Venerable Master Hsing Yun:
Life
For All Living Beings
Being Good
Humanistic Buddhism: A Blueprint for Life
Chan Heart, Chan Art
Between Ignorance and Enlightenment Series

Sutra Commentaries:
Four Insights for Finding Fulfillment:
   A Practical Guide to the Buddha's Diamond Sutra
The Rabbit's Horn:
   A Commentary on the Platform Sutra
The Universal Gate:
   A Commentary on Avalokitesvara's Universal Gate Sutra
The Great Realizations:
   A Commentary on the Eight Realizations
   of a Bodhisattva Sutra
Sutra of the Medicine Buddha

THE CORE TEACHINGS

Essays in Basic Buddhism

Venerable Master Hsing Yun

Buddha's Light Publishing, Los Angeles

© 2000, 2006, 2008, 2012 Buddha's Light Publishing
First edition 2000
Second edition 2006
Third edition 2008
Fourth edition 2012

By Venerable Master Hsing Yun
Translated and edited by Fo Guang Shan International Translation Center
Cover designed by Wilson Yau

Published by Buddha's Light Publishing
3456 S. Glenmark Drive,
Hacienda Heights, CA 91745, U.S.A.
Tel: (626) 923-5144
Fax: (626) 923-5145
E-mail: itc@blia.org
Website: www.blpusa.com

Printed in Taiwan.

Library of Congress Cataloging-in-Publication Data

Xingyun, da shi.
  The core teachings : essays in basic Buddhism / Venerable Master Hsing Yun. –
Fourth [edition].
     pages cm
  Translated and edited by Fo Guang Shan International Translation Center.

  ISBN 978-1-932293-68-5
  1. Buddhism–Doctrines. 2. Fo Guang Shan Buddhist Order–Doctrines. I. Fo
Guang Shan International Translation Center. II. Title.

  BQ9800.F6392X5549 2012
  294.3'42042--dc23

                                    2012012593

Contents

Acknowledgments

Like all of Buddha's Light Publishing's endeavors, this project benefited from the contributions of many people. We would like to thank Venerable Tzu Jung, the Chief Executive of the Fo Guang Shan International Translation Center (FGSITC), Venerble Hui Chi, Abbot of Hsi Lai Temple, and Venerable Yi Chao, Director of FGSITC for their support and leadership.

Pey-Rong Lee and Mu-Tzen Hsu provided the translation; John Gill edited the texts; Louvenia Ortega, Nathan Michon and Amanda Ling proofread the manuscript and prepared it for publication. The book was designed by Wan Kah Ong and the cover was designed by Wilson Yau. Portions of this edition were adapted from *Lotus in a Stream*, translated by Tom Graham.

Our appreciation goes to everyone who supported this project from conception to completion.

PUTTING TEACHINGS
INTO PRACTICE

There is one thing about the Dharma that I am completely sure of: the Dharma is for people. The Buddha's teachings are not a cold philosophy designed merely to rearrange the concepts in our minds, they are a living act of compassion intended to show us how to open our hearts. I learned this truth just as everyone must learn it—by living life and applying the Buddha's teachings to what I saw. I hope that by describing a few of my experiences, I will help readers understand my approach to the Dharma and why I feel so certain that the Dharma is something that must be practiced with other people, among other people, and for other people.

I was born in a country village in Jiangsu Province, China in 1928. Like most people of that time and place, my family held a mixture of religious beliefs; they believed in gods and spirits as well as in the teachings of the Buddha. Where one belief began and another left off was not always clear, but one thing was certain—religion was a very important part of everybody's life. By the time I was only three or four years old, I had already absorbed the deep religious convictions of my family.

During much of my boyhood, I lived in my maternal grand-mother's house. Due to her religious beliefs, my grandmother became a vegetarian at the age of eighteen. After she married my grandfather, she continued this practice and took up new ones. Every morning she awoke very early to chant. Though she could not read a single word, my grandmother had completely memorized both the *Amitabha Sutra* and the *Diamond Sutra*, among others. Her chanting brought her powerful religious experiences, which she interpreted as meaning that she was gaining supernatural powers. This caused her to redouble her efforts. She began getting up even earlier and meditating even more.

I can still remember her getting up in the middle of the night when it was still dark outside to meditate. Somewhere she had learned a yogic practice that made her stomach growl very loudly. The rumblings were so loud, they often woke me up out of my dreams.

Once I asked her, "Grandma, why does your stomach make so much noise?

She replied, "I've mastered my practice. It is the result of years of training."

In the years that followed, I was exposed to many other forms of popular religious practice, including séances, spirit walking, and visionary journeying into other realms.

I became a novice monk when I was twelve years old, and my world changed completely. I went from being a carefree child to being a disciplined student of the Dharma. I studied for seven or eight years before I went home again for the first time. By that time, the war with Japan was over. I found my grandmother sitting under a tree sewing. I knelt beside her and the thought came to me that in all the years I had been in the monastery I had not once heard anyone say anything about any meditation technique that would make your stomach growl. I thought that maybe this would be a good chance to teach my grandmother something more about the Dharma. I said, "Grandma, does your stomach still make that noise when you meditate?"

With the perfect sincerity of an old woman, she replied, "Of course it does. How could I possibly live without my practice?"

I said, "But what is the use of having your stomach growl? Cars and airplanes also make noise. A machine can make more noise than your stomach. Your stomach growling won't do anything to elevate humanity or liberate sentient beings from the cycle of birth and death. I have met many great masters over the last few years, and not one of them ever makes his stomach growl when he meditates."

My old grandmother was stunned by my words. She sat still for a long time. At last she said, "Then what is the right way to practice?"

I said, "We should practice by cultivating our moral character at every opportunity, and observing ourselves closely to learn the nature of the mind. None of this has anything to do with a growling stomach."

My grandmother looked at me for a long time. Beneath her kindly old gaze, my certitude dissolved completely. The worst thing was that she had believed me! Her decades of solitary practice were the foundation of her faith. Though it may have been true that the growling of her stomach was doing little for the morality of the human race, it was also true—and this was a far deeper truth—that her practice was all that she had. It had been everything to her. In a single thoughtless moment, and with just a few words, I had managed to cause her to doubt the very foundation of her faith. I could hardly bear to look upon the disappointment in her eyes. I was young and I had traveled beyond our little village, so she had believed me. We continued to talk, and yet I could see that nothing that I could say would ever remove the pain I had caused her. That memory troubles me to this day.

Before long, China entered the turmoil of civil war. I became part of a monastic relief team that was sent to Taiwan. At first, we all thought that we would return to mainland China very soon, but as the revolution progressed, and more troops retreated, we realized that we would probably have to stay in Taiwan for a long time. As I began to teach the Dharma in Taiwan, I remembered my experience with my grandmother. Never again did I try to destroy the complex folk beliefs that were held by the people who came to hear me speak. I had realized that this kind of religious conviction can be like an introduction to the higher truths taught by the Buddha. No one can comprehend the Dharma in a single sitting, and thus we should respect the beliefs that every person holds.

When I moved to Ilan on the east coast of Taiwan, I quickly realized that I was probably the first Buddhist monastic who had ever gone there to teach. There was a temple in the area dedicated to the goddess Matsu, a protector of sailors. Smoke from incense filled the temple all day long. All of the local people went there to bow before the altar and worship. None of those people had any real understanding of Buddhism, but they all thought that what they were doing was a form of Buddhist practice. Since they were satisfied with their religious practices, no one from outside had been able to convince them to try anything else. Many Christian missionaries had visited the area, but not one of them had succeeded in winning any converts.

With the memory of my grandmother's disappointment still fresh in my mind, I approached the task of presenting the Buddha's teachings with considerably more reserve than I might have. I decided that I would be gradual in my approach and carefully build upon what those people already had. I knew very well that to try to overturn their beliefs would do no one any good. Such a course of action would lead only to their disappointment in themselves or their rejection of the Dharma and me. Before the deep truths of the Buddha are widely disseminated within any society, it is important to go slow in teaching the Dharma. Wrong views are not as good as right views, but at least for a time they may serve to assuage the sense of loneliness and isolation that people feel when they have no religious conviction. My early years in the Chinese countryside taught me that religion is important for the well-being of society. One look in my grandmother's old eyes taught me to see that it is essential to the well-being of each and every human heart.

Every Buddhist monk has to study the Dharma and learn from as many teachers as he can, and I was no exception. My primary teacher was Master Zhikai, the abbot of Qixia Shan monastery, who ordained me as a novice monk. Qixia Shan monastery was one of the largest and oldest monasteries in China, and although Master Zhikai was well-respected as the abbot of such an institution, he did not offer me any special treatment. Like many monks of his generation, Master Zhikai was a harsh teacher. Work was hard and discipline was strict.

In the 1930s and 1940s, China was a very poor country. The monastery where I lived had over four hundred people living in it. Our community was so poor that we were served rice only about twice a month. The rest of the time we ate thin rice porridge. The porridge we were given for breakfast was so thin it was almost clear. The little bit of food that was served along with the porridge was usually nothing more than soybean remnants or dried turnip strips. Real tofu was reserved for guests. The turnip strips usually had maggots crawling out of them right at the table. Since we never had any cooking oil, the soybean dregs were never cooked. There were few nutrients in what we ate, but I don't remember people getting sick very often. Most of us were quite healthy. Monastic life taught us to be steadfast. We were expected to be tough and to be able to withstand physical hardship. Being steadfast is not the only virtue in the world, but I think that it can be very helpful in both learning and teaching the Dharma. If one cannot bear the trials of the body, then how can one ever expect to conquer the mind?

There is no better teacher than life itself. I don't like to teach my disciples that way anymore, but I do not regret having been trained in the old style. After you have spent years living like that, there is almost nothing that can ever disturb you again.

At fifteen I received full ordination. The ordination retreat lasted for fifty-three days. That period of time left an indelible impression on my mind. It is the source of many of the habits I still have today.

During the fifty-three days of the retreat we were required to pay absolute attention to what we were doing. For fifty-three days I barely opened my eyes, and I never once dared to turn my head and look at what was going on around me. At fifteen, most children are very curious about their surroundings. They want to look at everything and see who is doing what. If they hear the wind in the grass, they want to go to the window and see what is going on. This is the normal curiosity of a young person. During my ordination, such behavior was impermissible. If we moved out of place, one of the presiding monks would come over with his willow stick and beat us quite severely. He would say, "Little boy, what do you think you're doing? Pull your ears in and quit paying so much attention to things outside of yourself!" Or, "Young man, don't keep looking around at everything you see! Of all the things that you see, which of them belong to you?"

I can well remember being hit by that stick and then thinking that what the master had said was true: in all of Qixia Shan monastery, there was not a brick, or a tile, or a blade of grass anywhere that belonged to me. That lesson really sank in, and today I still have the habit of often closing my eyes and withdrawing from the world around me. The peaceful vistas of the inner world open up, and my eyes and ears are filled with the sound of inner solitude rather than the noise of the outside world. When the ordination retreat was almost over and I got my first look at the world again, I can still remember how vivid and fresh it appeared to me. Mountains and trees and flowers leapt into my mind with an intensity I had never experienced before.

There is a saying, "Talking about the Dharma for ten minutes is not as valuable as practicing it for one minute." The essays in this book have been presented to help people learn the profound teachings of Sakyamuni Buddha. They have not been presented as mere ideas, to be held apart from life. To learn the Dharma and not practice it would be tragic! It is my greatest hope that everyone who reads this book will also practice the teachings contained within it. Chanting the Buddha's name or being consistent about meditation is like cooking. Our effort should be consistent, like the fire under a pot of rice. If we light the stove and then turn it off again, we will not succeed in preparing our meal. But if we apply the right amount of heat for the correct length of time, we will benefit from our effort. This is the wisdom of thousands of years of Buddhist practice. When we focus on these teachings and allow ourselves to be receptive to them, our lives will be filled with compassion and we will learn the way to the truth.

Buddhist practice must start with who we are and what we do. First we learn to control the negative impulses of the body. This is morality. Then we learn to control the mind. This is meditation. Then we learn to understand the deep truths of life. This is wisdom. Each stage depends on the one before it. When I was a young man we spent many long hours meditating. Like many Chinese monasteries, Qixia Shan Monastery taught a mixture of Pure Land and Chan teachings. Sometimes we chanted Amitabha Buddha's name and sometimes we simply meditated on the Buddha nature within us. These two practices fit together quite well because the first teaches us to be humble enough to rely on the Buddha, while the second teaches us to be wise enough to rely on ourselves.

We usually meditated at night when I was in the monastery. I suppose that part of the reason was that we had nothing else to do. Our temple was situated deep in the mountains and we had very few resources. It would have been out of the question to waste lamp oil for reading in the evening when we didn't even have enough oil for use in our food.

We were taught to sit in the lotus position, with our legs crossed and each foot on top of the opposite thigh. The purpose of meditation is to make the mind tranquil so that the distraction of deluded thinking can settle. As these thoughts settle, a higher awareness begins to appear. In Buddhist writings, the mind is sometimes compared to a pool of water. Its original nature is clear and pure, and it becomes cloudy only when the silt of delusion is stirred up in it. Meditation is a way of letting the silt in the pool settle. Once it has settled, everything becomes clear. Probably the greatest lesson that we can learn from sitting meditation is that mental clarity can also be achieved in all other situations. Once we become accomplished at sitting meditation, we will begin to see that it is possible to meditate while standing, or walking, or doing just about anything.

Meditation is an essential part of Buddhist practice, but no one should think that meditation is all that there is to Buddhism. The deepest truth that I learned in the meditation hall at Qixia Shan monastery is that the mind in meditation is the mind of all sentient beings, and that it is the mind of all Buddhas. Meditation is a door; what goes through the door is our compassion for others.

The biggest single reason that people do not gain much from their practice or drop it entirely is that they do not properly balance practice and learning. Due to this imbalance, they lose heart and conclude that there is nothing to be gained from the Dharma. If our understanding of the Dharma is based only on words or ideas, we will not have deep understanding. The purpose of chanting and meditation is to show us that the insights of the Buddha are *real*. When we experience them in meditation, or when we are inspired by them in chanting, we renew ourselves and empower ourselves to continue the long process of introspection and moral growth that is the path to awakening. If you feel yourself lagging in your studies or becoming bored with the Dharma, find a good place to meditate, or seek out an opportunity to join a retreat. You will be transformed by the experience. With practice the benefits of meditation can be brought into the mind very quickly. With practice we learn to see the Buddha within, and not to look outside.

My single greatest ambition has always been to disseminate the Dharma through writing. Only the written word survives the ages. I learned the Dharma largely from the writings of others and

I feel that it is my duty to try to pass it on in good condition. The truths contained in the Dharma transcend language, and yet the medium that people use for conveying those truths is language. I hope that readers of this small book will enjoy the words that follow as they profit from the deep wisdom of the Buddha.

Chapter One

THE LIFE OF THE BUDDHA

B uddhism originated in India over 2,500 years ago and has
spread throughout most of Asia where it has had a tremen-
dous influence on religion, culture, philosophy, and psychology.
Within the last century, its popularity has spread to the West, particularly Europe and the United States.

Buddhism is the name given to the practice of the teachings of Sakyamuni Buddha. The Sanskrit word *Buddha* means
"awakened one," and refers to those who have awakened to the
Dharma, the truth. The historical founder of Buddhism was an
Indian prince of the Sakya clan named Siddhartha Gautama.
After his awakening he was known as *Sakyamuni*, "sage of the
Sakyans." Sakyamuni Buddha's teachings on the truth of reality and how to awaken to one's intrinsic nature are as relevant
today as they were in his time. However, before we discuss the
teachings of the Buddha in depth, let us look at the life of the man
whose quest for truth continues to be the model for those seeking
an end to suffering.

THE LIFE OF THE BUDDHA

Before Sakyamuni Buddha was born on earth and became a Buddha for the sake of all sentient beings, he spent countless lives as a "bodhisattva," one who is practicing to become a Buddha. For many lifetimes, the bodhisattva diligently practiced and cultivated, developing the virtues of Buddhahood. In his penultimate birth, the bodhisattva was born into Tusita Heaven, where he waited for conditions to be right in the human realm for him to appear in the world and become the next Buddha. When the conditions for his rebirth were right, the bodhisattva entered the womb of his earthly mother, Queen Maya.

It was around 500 BCE when the bodhisattva took his final rebirth. The kingdom of Kapilavastu, in present-day southern Nepal, was ruled by the Sakyas. The bodhisattva's father, Suddhodana, was king of the Sakyas, and his mother, Maya, was a princess of Devadaha.

At the end of spring, on the eighth day of the fourth lunar month, a prince was born in Lumbini Garden. It is said that in the first moments after his birth, he took seven steps and, with one hand pointing toward the sky and the other pointing toward the earth, said, "This is my final rebirth in this world. I have appeared in this world to become a Buddha. I will realize the truth of the universe. I will liberate sentient beings everywhere." The prince was named Siddhartha, which means "accomplishing all."

As was the custom, King Suddhodana summoned the most learned of wise men to foretell his son's destiny. One of the prince's first visitors was a renowned sage named Asita who predicted that Siddhartha would become a great king of the world if he remained a layperson, or he would become a Buddha who liberates sentient beings if he left the home life. On the seventh day after Siddhartha's birth, Queen Maya died. Her sister, Queen Mahaprajapati, lovingly raised the child as her own.

From an early age, it was quite evident that the young prince was extremely bright and that he excelled in all things. By the time Siddhartha was twelve years old, he was adept at the classical "five sciences" of composition, mathematics, medicine, logic, and philosophy and excelled at the study of the four *Vedas*. In addition to his abilities in a wide range of scholarly subjects, he was also an adept warrior who was skilled in the martial arts.

The prince grew into a young man who was greatly admired for his strength, intelligence, dignity, and beauty. When Siddhartha reached marrying age, King Suddhodana arranged for his son to take a wife. Yasodhara, the beautiful daughter of a Sakya nobleman, was chosen.

Still, King Suddhodana feared that Prince Siddhartha might leave the palace and his royal position. To prevent his son from leaving, King Suddhodana sheltered him from the world by building him special pleasure palaces and surrounding him with beautiful women, music, wine, and other luxuries. Nevertheless, these worldly pleasures of the palace could not satisfy the feelings of loneliness that had crept into the prince's heart.

One day, Siddhartha went to tell his father that he wished to travel outside the palace walls to see the kingdom. Hearing this, King Suddhodana immediately ordered that the kingdom be decorated and cleared of anything unpleasant. Furthermore, the elderly, the sick, the ascetics, and corpses were not permitted near the prince lest they arouse feelings that disturbed his mind.

On his first journey, the prince and Chandaka, his personal charioteer, saw a frail-looking man who was bent over with age.

Siddhartha, shocked by the sight, asked Chandaka about the old man and discovered that old age was a part of the human condition. The prince was so upset that he asked to be taken back to the palace.

During his second outing, Siddhartha encountered a man who was extremely sick. The prince again looked to Chandaka for answers. When Chandaka explained that all people fall ill at some point in their lives, the prince became deeply troubled. Unable to continue onward, the prince returned to the palace with a heavy heart.

The third time they went driving in the chariot, Siddhartha and Chandaka came upon a funeral procession. The prince watched as grief-stricken relatives carried a lifeless body through the streets. Some mourners wept softly while others openly wailed in suffering. Distressed by the spectacle, the prince wished to know why people had to die. Chandaka explained that no one could escape death and everything that is born must one day die. Siddhartha then contemplated all that he had seen, and lamented the realization that life was impermanent.

On a fourth and final journey, Siddhartha and Chandaka encountered an ascetic who walked towards them. The prince stood up to receive him and asked about his unusual clothing. The man explained that he had renounced the world to seek liberation from the suffering of old age, sickness, and death. After Siddhartha heard these words, his heart filled with joy and his mind gave rise to the thought of taking up the life of a wandering ascetic.

These visions beyond his life of contentment left an indelible impression on Siddhartha. His father noticed the change in him and desperately tried to divert him with more music, beautiful women, feasts, and fine things. However, Siddhartha could not be deterred from his resolve to leave the worldly life behind.

In the prince's twenty-ninth year of life, his wife bore him a son, Rahula. Not long afterward, the prince decided to leave the palace to seek liberation from old age, sickness, and death. With one last look at his sleeping wife and infant son, Siddhartha vowed that he would return to see them when he had awakened to the truth. As everyone slept, he rode away from Kapilavastu with faithful Chandaka by his side.

When they reached a serene forest outside the city, the prince took off his fine silken clothing and removed his jeweled ornaments. Handing them to Chandaka, Siddhartha told his attendant to return with the horse to Kapilavastu. Then, with his sword, he cut off his long hair and severed all attachments to his old life.

For the next six years, Siddhartha—who now went by his family name, Gautama—sought out teachers in order to learn how to be free from old age, sickness, and death. Since he had entered the life of an ascetic, Gautama followed the practices of fasting and meditating under extreme conditions of hardship and deprivation. After six years had passed in this way, Gautama was near death. He realized that complete liberation still eluded him, so he abandoned asceticism.

From there, he made his way to Nairanjana where he bathed the filth from his body. As Gautama meditated beneath a banyan tree, he was given an offering of milk rice from the maiden Sujata. When his strength returned, he traveled to Bodhgaya where he seated himself beneath a tree that would later be known as the "bodhi tree," and began to meditate. He swore that he would not stir from his seat, even at the cost of his life, until he had liberated himself from the cycle of birth and death and attained awakening.

Sitting in meditation, Gautama conquered the demons of his mind—greed, anger, and ignorance—as well as Mara, the king of the demons. After defeating Mara, Gautama entered a deep meditative state called *samadhi*. Through this deep contemplation, he first saw all of his countless past lives. Then, he realized the non-duality of birth and death. He saw sentient beings within the six realms of existence suffering endlessly from karmic cause and effect. In the third realization, he came to understand dependent origination. Even after he realized the truth of the universe, Gautama continued to meditate and contemplate under the bodhi tree for twenty-one days.

At the first light of dawn, Gautama finally awakened to the root of suffering—ignorance. Thus, he found the way leading to the cessation of this suffering. Forty-nine days after he had made his vow, on the eighth day of the twelfth lunar month under a night sky filled with stars, Gautama attained complete awakening. He was thirty-five years old. From this moment forth, he was known as Sakyamuni Buddha.

After his awakening, the Buddha spent forty-nine years teaching the Dharma. At the age of eighty, on the fifteenth day of the second lunar month, under a pair of sala trees, the Buddha entered final *nirvana*. The legacy he left his disciples was profound, for the Buddha had dedicated his earthly life to teaching others the Four Noble Truths, dependent origination, karma, the three Dharma seals, emptiness, the Noble Eightfold Path, the five precepts, the six perfections, and the Middle Way. Ever since Sakyamuni Buddha transmitted the Dharma to his disciples, countless sentient beings through the centuries have heard the teachings, cultivated the path, and attained awakening.

Chapter Two

HOW TO STUDY
BUDDHISM

When the Buddha taught the Dharma, he gave the world an inexhaustible gift: the ability to find true freedom. The Dharma is a mirror that reflects the truth within us and shows us how to free ourselves from our own delusions. This truth is the same truth that governs the universe. As we examine our minds in the mirror of the Buddha's teachings, we will discover a certain wisdom that has always been present.

The value of learning the Dharma is not something that can be easily measured. The first step we must take when we enter the gate of the Dharma is to look at ourselves. We must decide that we want to change, that we want to learn, and that we will really try to apply the Buddha's teachings in our daily lives. The moment we embrace the Dharma, our lives will begin to change. The Dharma is like a light that dispels the darkness.

The process of learning the Dharma is the most exciting and wonderful kind of self-discovery. In the sections below, I will try to explain how to approach and practice the Dharma.

THE FOUR RELIANCES

The truths that the Buddha taught are fundamental truths, which mean that they are true everywhere and at all times. As Buddhist practitioners searching for the Dharma, we must rely on four guidelines to keep us on the right path. These "four reliances" are to rely on the Dharma, not on an individual teacher; rely on wisdom, not on knowledge; rely on the meaning, not on the words; and rely on ultimate truth, not on relative truth.

Rely on the Dharma, Not on an Individual Teacher

To rely on the Dharma is to always rely on the truth. We cannot rely on people because everyone has different perceptions and interpretations. Any single teacher is subject to birth, aging, sickness, and death, but the Dharma has not changed since beginningless time. So in seeking the Way, we must always rely on the Dharma itself and not on the people who teach it.

Although there are people who can instruct us and help us along the path, we still must experience and understand it for ourselves in order to truly make it our own. When learning from others, we should examine everything under the lens of our own introspection. In a famous Chan story, a student once asked Chan Master Zhaozhou (778-897) how to learn the Dharma. Master Zhaozhou stood up and said, "I am going to go take a piss now. Ah, even trivial matters like taking a piss I must do myself."

Sakyamuni Buddha once said that we should rely on ourselves and rely on the Dharma, not on others. We should believe in ourselves, rely on ourselves, believe in the Dharma, and rely on the Dharma. Therefore, while we should listen to the teachings of the Buddha and the instructions of our teachers, if we truly wish to gain wisdom we still must rely on ourselves to experience the truth.

Rely on Wisdom, Not on Knowledge

What is the difference between wisdom and knowledge? Wisdom is the truth that already lies within us. Knowledge is what we have gained through our experiences in the outside world.

So why must we rely on wisdom and not on knowledge? The knowledge that we acquire through our six sense organs (eyes, ears, nose, tongue, body, and mind) is constantly shifting with the changes of phenomena. This is why knowledge is not perfect. On the other hand, wisdom is like a mirror of our true nature. When we use this mirror to look at all the phenomena of the universe, it will reflect things as they really are. As we walk down the path of cultivation, if we can see the reality of all things with our wisdom and not discriminate based on our knowledge, we will not be deluded by the illusions of the world.

Rely on Meaning, Not on Words

We often gain knowledge and realize the truth through the medium of language and words. While there are many different languages throughout the world, the truth that they express is essentially the same. By realizing this, we can seek to grasp the essential meaning of things rather than being mired in the words. If we are too attached to words, we end up with a superficial understanding and will not comprehend something's real meaning.

The unusual behavior of Chan masters was calculated to open our minds to this point. In one story, a Chan master exclaimed, "Today, if I saw Sakyamuni Buddha teach the Dharma, I'd beat him to death with a stick and feed him to the dogs!" Another master said, "What of the sacred texts? Bring them here and I'll use them as a rag!"

The wild words of the Chan masters may seem to slander the Buddha and the Dharma, but in fact, they want us to transcend the attachment to language and words, and realize the truth beyond them.

Rely on Ultimate Truth, Not on Relative Truth

When we say, "rely on ultimate truth," this means that we rely on the definitive meaning and not on the various methods of teaching. Buddhism has divided into different traditions in order to teach the Dharma to as many sentient beings as possible. Within these traditions, many different schools have been established based on various methods of cultivation.

The various methods that the Buddha taught us are all "skillful means," because they are tailored to the different needs and capacities of sentient beings. However, we cannot consider these skillful means as the ultimate way to learn the Dharma since they are relative truth, and they change with the person and the conditions. According to the Buddha, the ultimate way is to follow the definitive meaning of the Dharma, which is in accordance with the Buddha mind.

THE FOUR STATES OF MIND
FOR STUDYING THE DHARMA

What state of mind should Buddhist practitioners have when they study the Dharma? To be able to receive the teachings, we must possess a mind with faith, a mind that questions, a mind of awakening, and finally, no mind at all.

Faith

We study Buddhism to purify and calm the body and mind, elevate our character, open up our world, and give us direction. Buddhism can help us discover that we are in charge of the mind. On this path to self-discovery, faith plays an important role.

Dr. Sun Yat-sen (1866-1925), regarded as the Father of the Republic of China, once said, "Faith is strength." The *Treatise on the Perfection of Great Wisdom* says, "The Dharma is as vast as the ocean. It can only be entered with faith." The *Flower Adornment Sutra* says, "Faith is the origin of the Way and the mother of all virtue. It nourishes the roots of goodness."

There is a story in Buddhism that illustrates how faith gives us strength. In the countryside, there was a little old lady who wished to learn the Dharma. Unfortunately, there was no one around to teach her. One day, a layman who did not have a good grasp of Buddhism came to this village. When he saw how much the little old lady wanted to learn the Dharma, he said, "I know a Buddhist mantra I can teach to you: 'Om mani padme *um*.'" The layman had made a mistake, and mispronounced the last syllable as "*um*," rather than "hum."

The old lady did not know any better, so every day, she chanted "Om mani padme *um*." Each time she chanted the mantra, she would pick up a bean and place it in a bowl. After many years of chanting in this way, she did not need to pick up the beans anymore. Whenever she chanted "Om mani padme *um*" in her mind, the beans would jump into the bowl on their own.

Several years later, a monastic was wandering through the village and heard the old lady chanting "Om mani padme *um*." The monastic informed her that she had been chanting incorrectly, and that the correct mantra was "Om mani padme hum."

The old lady thought, "Oh dear! I have been chanting wrong all these years!" Afterwards, she chanted the mantra correctly, with "hum," but the beans no longer jumped into the bowl by themselves.

Whether we chant "hum" or "um" is unimportant. As long as we have faith, our faith will give us strength. Faith is as important to us as roots to a tree: without it we cannot accomplish anything, for it gives us our strength. As Buddhist practitioners, we should study the Dharma with a mindset of faith and sincerity.

Questioning

In what state of mind should Buddhist practitioners approach the Dharma? Perhaps many of you have doubts and questions? The Buddha taught that we should study the Dharma with a questioning mind. This is how Buddhism differs from other religions, for in addition to emphasizing faith, it also tells us to doubt. In the Chan School of Buddhism, practitioners are encouraged to doubt and ask questions. This is why they say in the Chan School, "Small doubts lead to small awakenings. Great doubts lead to great awakenings. No doubt leads to no awakening."

The Dharma is like a bell. If you tap it gently it will ring softly. If you strike it hard it will resound loudly. However, if you do not strike it at all, it will not ring. We must have questions in order to gain answers. In fact, the Buddhist sutras themselves are largely the questions of disciples, which the Buddha answers.

Chan Buddhism instructs practitioners to question and investigate. This method is called *huatou*, which literally means "speech head," or essential words. For hundreds of years, Chan masters have used this method to achieve awakening. As a result, much of Chan literature is the pithy exchange of questions and answers between Chan masters and their students. These exchanges are often profound and difficult for most people to understand. In a Chan meditation hall you are likely to hear such questions as, "What was your original face before you were born?" "What is the meaning of Bodhidharma coming from the west?" and "Who is it that chants the Buddha's name?" This questions require us to doubt, and from these doubts we can gain wisdom and awaken to the truth.

Awakening

People go to school to gain knowledge. People study the Dharma to awaken. Awakening is not the process of accumulating knowledge; it is a moment of sudden realization. It is when we think, "Ah ha! I understand." How then, do we reach the state of awakening?

Once there was a young student who went to ask a Chan master, "I just came to the monastery and do not understand anything. Master, please instruct me: how do I enter the Way?"

The Chan master replied, "Do you hear the birds singing in the trees? The crickets chirping? Can you see the water flowing in the stream? The flowers blooming?"

The young student replied, "Yes!"

Then the Chan master told him, "The Way is entered from all these things."

We can see that the Dharma is not mysterious, nor is it separate from our lives. It is always a part of the world around us. When we "understand" the sound of the flowing water, that is the sound of the Buddha's voice. When we see flowers blooming, it is the presence of the Buddha. When we awaken to the truth, everything we do is the Way. We do not need to go far away in search of the Way, for it is in our lives and in our minds.

There is another story that illustrates this point. Once a novice monk named Longtan went to study under Chan Master Tianhuang (748-807). Year after year passed, but Chan Master Tianhuang never gave any formal instruction. Longtan finally became frustrated and went to bid farewell to Chan Master Tianhuang. Surprised by this, Tianhuang said to him, "Where are you going?"

Longtan said, "I am going elsewhere to learn the Dharma."

Chan Master Tianhuang replied, "There is the Dharma right here. Why do you need to go somewhere else to study?"

Longtan replied, "I've been here for a long time. Why have you never taught me the Dharma?"

Chan Master Tianhuang said, "When you bring me tea, I use my hands to take it from you. When you bring me food, I use my mouth to eat it. When you bow to me, I nod to you. When have I not taught the Dharma to you?"

Longtan bowed his head in thought.

Tianhuang then said, "Don't think. Once you think, you've gone astray. You need to experience and directly bear responsibility."

With these words, Longtan suddenly had a great awakening.

Actually, the Dharma is in our every action, just as Chan is in every flower, tree, and stone. We usually do not realize that the Dharma is in our mind, so we look for it outside of ourselves. Yet, the more we seek, the farther away we go. The Dharma teaches us that we must always look within. If we can do this, the Way will become very close to us.

No-Mind

Wuxin (無心) or "no-mind" is a Chinese expression to refer to a mind that is empty of discrimination. It is the true mind, and transcends the duality of existence and non-existence. When we study the Dharma we cannot approach it with a discriminating mind, because discrimination and differentiation are based on knowledge, and knowledge is constantly changing. "No-mind" is a mind that does not differentiate. Only with this kind of wisdom can we deeply penetrate the truths of the Dharma.

In the past, someone asked a Chan master, "Master, you usually meditate for a very long time. May I ask: do you enter *samadhi* with mind or no-mind?"

The Chan master answered, "When I enter *samadhi*, it is neither with mind nor with no-mind. I enter it with the mind that is beyond all duality."

When we talk about this mind that transcends duality, it does not mean that we do not have any concept of right and wrong, or good and bad. We should have these concepts. However, in dealing with worldly affairs and dualities, we need to face them with the non-differentiating mind, the mind of wisdom.

Once a student asked Chan Master Guishan (771-853), "What is the Way?"

Chan Master Guishan replied, "No-mind is the Way."

The student said, "I don't know how!"

Guishan replied, "Go find someone who knows how."

The student said, "Who knows how?"

The master said, "It is not someone else. It is you!"

No-mind allows us to see the world as it really is, not as our discriminating mind tells us it is. By applying no-mind to the world around us, we will gain the clarity to see the Buddha in everything and our Buddha nature within.

Chapter Three

DEPENDENT ORIGINATION

While sitting underneath the bodhi tree, the Buddha gazed up at the stars and attained awakening. The truth that he awakened to was the universal truth of dependent origination, one of the central teachings of Buddhism. Dependent origination is also the most significant characteristic that distinguishes Buddhism from other philosophies and religions.

What is dependent origination? "Dependent origination" states that no phenomena can arise from nothing, nor can they exist by themselves independently. Phenomena come into existence when the causes and conditions are right. The *Commentary on the Surangama Sutra* states, "All teachings, from the simplest to the most profound, say that phenomena do not exist outside of causes and conditions."

DEPENDENT ORIGINATION AND
CAUSES AND CONDITIONS

Everything in this world comes into being because of causes and conditions. Without the proper causes and conditions, no phenomena would arise, and nothing could exist.

Stated simply like this, the truth of dependent origination may seem obvious or trivial, yet it has far-reaching consequences, for it means that nothing has an independent existence of its own. There is no "self" that exists separately from others. It also means that there is no absolute phenomenon anywhere in the universe. Since all phenomena are interdependent, if the causes and conditions that produce or sustain a phenomenon are removed, that phenomenon will cease to exist.

The Buddha said, "All phenomena arise from causes and conditions. All phenomena disappear due to causes and conditions." But what are "causes and conditions"? Where do they come from? Causes and conditions themselves are phenomena, and they arise from other causes and conditions.

Some phenomena are labeled "causes" and others are labeled "conditions" to help us understand how phenomena arise and cease. But these terms only mean something in relationship to one another. What is considered a "cause" in one instance may be considered a "condition" in another. It all depends on from what angle these phenomena are observed.

Cause and condition are the two basic factors that produce or underlie each and every phenomenon in the universe. The more powerful primary factor that leads to the arising of the phenomenon is called the "cause," while the secondary factors are called "conditions."

For example, a seed that is planted in the soil needs water, fertilizer, air, and sunlight to grow. The seed is the cause. The soil, water, fertilizer, air, and sunlight are conditions. Only when all of the right causes and conditions are present will there be the result of a healthy plant. Without a cause, there could be no effect. With a cause but no conditions, there would also be no effect. When both the cause and conditions come together, that will produce an effect.

Dependent origination is not something invented by the Buddha. It is a universal principle underlying all phenomena in the universe. When the Buddha attained awakening, he realized this principle. After his awakening, the Buddha taught others what he had come to understand. He taught that if we contemplate the concept of causes and conditions from the perspective of sentient beings trapped within the cycle of birth and death, we should be able to see that our lives have not been created by some god that stands outside of the universe, but rather that our lives are the result of a complex interaction of causes and conditions.

DEPENDENT ORIGINATION AND CAUSE AND EFFECT

In the section above, we moved toward an understanding of dependent origination by focusing on the causes and conditions that produce all phenomena in the universe. In this section, we will deepen our understanding of dependent origination by focusing on the interactions of cause and effect. Cause and effect is a fundamental principle that underlies all phenomena. Every phenomenon is caused by other phenomena and every phenomenon also produces effects.

The *Samyukta Agama* says, "This exists, therefore, that exists. This arises, therefore, that arises. This is absent, therefore, that is absent. This is extinguished, therefore, that is extinguished."

The "this" and "that" mentioned above refer to cause and effect. This quote implies that neither cause nor effect has an independent nature. They both exist together in a state of dynamic interaction. Without one, the other could not be. Just as the words "cause" and "condition" are relative terms, so are the words "cause" and "effect." In reality, this universe is an extremely intricate and complicated web of dynamically interrelated phenomena. The Buddha used the words "cause," "condition," "effect," and "result" to help us understand some of the general features of this web of phenomena. It is important for each one of us to try to understand this universe because this is where we live. We are a part of it, and what we think about it has great influence both on ourselves and on other sentient beings.

When it comes to cause and effect, there is no "first cause" and no "last effect." This is because the present cause contains many previous causes. Following this logic, there is no beginning. Likewise, after the present effect, more effects will follow. Because of this, there is no ultimate "end."

Cause and effect are related, but the roles they play are not absolute. Causes produce effects, but those effects in turn produce other effects, and in doing so, become causes. Causes and effects are really interlocking parts of an endless chain of events. Something may be a cause from one point of view, but an effect from another.

Cause and effect are spread across the past, present, and future. Sometimes it is hard for us to understand and accept that all our intentional behavior produces effects. We cannot hide from the consequence of our own actions. We may wait ten million years, but one day, when the conditions are right, the effects of our choices can still manifest.

Cause and effect are always joined, like two sides of the same coin. Every cause contains effects just as every effect contains a cause. If you plant a bean, you will not harvest a melon. If you intentionally perform a bad deed, you will not reap a reward.

To arrive at a better understanding of dependent origination, let us examine six of its key principles one at a time:

1. Effects Arise from Causes

Dependent origination first depends on the presence of a cause and then on the right conditions before the effect can manifest. If there is no cause, there can be no effect. If there is a cause, but conditions are not right, then there also will be no effect. A "cause" phenomenon is a primary, direct requirement to produce an effect. A "condition" phenomena is an external, indirect requirement to help a cause to produce an effect.

For example, all human beings have the "seed," the necessary cause, to become Buddhas within them. But if this is not supported by good conditions like studying the Dharma, upholding the precepts, and so forth, then the effect of Buddhahood will not arise. Similarly, a person who has the latent cause of anger within him may be able to control his anger for many years. However, if the conditions are right, such a person may suddenly explode seemingly without reason. As you can see, the cause is the primary requirement for an effect, while conditions are secondary requirements.

All phenomena in the universe are governed by causes and conditions. Nothing exists outside of this relationship.

2. Phenomena Are Temporary

From the above principle, we know that all phenomena do not arise by themselves, but arise due to causes and conditions. In the same way, all phenomena cease due to causes and conditions. Because of this, all phenomena merely appear temporarily, and do not have any substantial existence of their own. As they have no substantial existence, phenomena appear when the right conditions arise, and disappear when the right conditions cease. This is the meaning of the Buddhist saying, "All things arise from dependent origination, all things' nature is emptiness."

3. Events Depend on Principles

Phenomena arise due to causes and conditions, but they also do so in a way that is consistent with principles. For example, if you plant a pumpkin seed, you will not reap a tomato. Causes of a certain type produce effects that are consistent with that type. This is a certain truth, and there is no event that occurs outside of principles.

4. Many Come from One

To most people, "one" is "one," and "many" is "many." But in Buddhism, "one" is "many" and "many" is "one," and furthermore, "many" come from "one." Most people do not look at the world in this way, and as such they do not reap the benefits of Buddhist practice. Such people cannot see the potential that lies within things, especially the potential within the human mind. A seed may grow into a tree that produces many fruits, so one can say that much fruit can come from a single seed. Likewise, a single small act of kindness may create many ripples that change the world for the better, and one small act of intentional cruelty may cause many destructive results that could last for a long time.

5. Existence Relies on Emptiness

The principles that have been previously discussed, such as "effects arise from causes" and "events depend on principles" have to do with existing phenomena. In Buddhism, existence itself is said to be dependent on "emptiness," which means that no phenomena has an independent existence. Since all things are interconnected, not one of them can be said to have a permanent, substantial existence. All things have this emptiness as their nature, and their very existence depends on this emptiness.

An example that is commonly used to explain this point is that of the wooden table. A table comes from a tree, and the tree depends on the conditions of soil, water, and sunshine to grow. Even though a table appears to have some substantial existence, it actually relies on many different conditions coming together so that it may arise temporarily. Aside from the external conditions that gave rise to the tree, someone had to cut the tree, move it, make the table, and put it in your room. As soon as we begin to investigate the causes and conditions on which the table depends for its existence, we find that ultimately there is no "table nature." Rather, what makes the table is an endlessly complex web of interconnectedness, impermanence, and change. If even one element is removed from that web, there might not be a table at all.

None of this says that the table does not exist. It means that the nature of a table is empty. If the nature of phenomena were not empty, then it would have no value. This is what emptiness does: it gives things value and purpose. The value and function of a table belongs to conventional reality. The "emptiness" of the table belongs to ultimate reality.

Understanding emptiness requires that we understand the impermanence and interconnectedness of all things. When we understand that all things are impermanent and interconnected, then we can understand that not one of them has its own substantial existence.

The great Buddhist philosopher, Nagarjuna, said, "Because there is emptiness, all phenomena exist. Without emptiness, all phenomena could not be." This is to say, all things rely on emptiness for their very existence.

6. A Buddha Comes from a Human Being

When Sakyamuni Buddha awakened, he said, "All sentient beings have the Tathagata's wisdom and virtue, but they fail to realize it because they cling to deluded thoughts and attachments." The Buddha said time and again that all of us have Buddha nature and that anyone who works long and hard enough at purifying his or her mind will eventually become a Buddha as well. Our attachments are like dark clouds that conceal the brightness of the moon or like mud that obscures a pond's clear water.

In our study of Buddhism, we must understand the cycle of birth and death and the truth that "This is absent, therefore, that is absent. This ceases, therefore that ceases," so we can put an end to our ignorance and reveal our Buddha nature. In this way we can attain the state of non-duality, the state without the limitations of space and time, or birth and death. This is awakening.

There is a saying in Buddhism, "A Buddha is an awakened sentient being. Sentient beings are unawakened Buddhas." The *Sutra on the Principles of the Six Perfections* says, "All sentient beings enter the wisdom of the Buddha by purifying the mind. The nature of a Buddha is no different from that of any other sentient being."

FOUR KINDS OF CONDITIONS

Dependent origination is the interplay between causes, conditions, and effects. Although causes are primary, conditions are also very important. Rather than have a single dominant cause, effects can be generated by the coming together of many conditions. There are four basic kinds of conditions that are related to our discussion of dependent origination. They are as follows:

1. Causal Conditions

This refers to those conditions which most directly act as causes to produce an effect. For example, the seed that produces a seedling is considered to be the causal condition for that seed.

2. Comparable Uninterrupted Conditions

Comparable uninterrupted conditions refer to a string of conditions where each condition acts as the seed of the next condition. As each condition arises and ceases, another similar condition is created in a constant series without gap or interruption. Comparable uninterrupted conditions can be seen most clearly in the mind. When the mind encounters an object, it produces thought. Previous thought creates present thought, and present thought creates future thought. Each thought conditions the next in conjunction with other conditions to create a thought that is similar, but different. All of these thoughts also interact with other conditions.

3. Object Conditions

All external objects which influence the mind are called object conditions. For example, forms seen by the eye create eye-consciousness, which acts as an object condition upon the mind.

Object conditions also interact with the stream of comparable uninterrupted conditions described above. Past, present, and future phenomena are also object conditions which act upon the mind.

4. Advancing Conditions

All other conditions that help or do not hinder the arising of phenomena are called advancing conditions.

The four kinds of conditions discussed above can also be thought of as being either "direct" or "indirect." All causal conditions operate directly on phenomena, while the other three kinds of conditions operate indirectly.

When looking more deeply into the four kinds of conditions, we see that matter only requires causal conditions and advancing conditions to function. The mind, in contrast, requires all four conditions to operate.

DEPENDENT ORIGINATION AND HUMAN LIFE

Dependent origination shows us the relationship between the arising, changing, and ceasing of phenomena, as well as the origin of human suffering. If we ignore or discount the fact that all things are impermanent and change due to causes and conditions, we are setting ourselves up to suffer. Whenever we ignore the reality of dependent origination and are attached to the delusion of permanence, we bring suffering onto ourselves. In contrast, when we are mindful of the forces that affect the phenomenal world, we prepare ourselves to deal with them in a positive and productive manner. If we understand that many are born from one and that all conditions are caused, then we will understand how to bring about good conditions in our own lives and in the world.

A true understanding of dependent origination will bring us joy, for it teaches us that the future lies in our own hands. Future conditions depend on causal seeds that we plant today. Liberation is achieved through practicing and understanding this truth, and for the benefit of all sentient beings. A clear understanding of dependent origination strengthens the mind because it teaches us how to understand what is most valuable in life and how to turn negative circumstances into positive ones.

Dependent origination teaches us that nothing in the world is permanent and explains why this is so. To understand dependent origination is to understand that all phenomena are conditioned by other phenomena and that all of them "rely on emptiness." Nothing has a substantial existence, including us. Ultimately, we too are empty. Clear understanding of this truth leads to liberation into a reality that lies beyond greed, anger, ignorance, attachment, suffering, and all delusions of duality.

Frequent contemplation of dependent origination can inspire us to be grateful for the things we have and the world we live in. It can teach us how to flow with life in a way that benefits both ourselves and others. Dependent origination gives us hope as it shows us how to understand the deepest meaning of life. The *Rice Stalk Sutra* says, "To see dependent origination is to see the Dharma. To see the Dharma is to see the Buddha."

Chapter Four

THE FOUR NOBLE TRUTHS

When Sakyamuni Buddha attained awakening, he saw that the entire universe functions in accordance with the truth of dependent origination. When he decided to teach others what he had realized, the Buddha knew that if he explained dependent origination directly to them, it would be difficult for them to understand, and it might even cause them to become afraid. For this reason, in his first teachings, the Buddha taught the Four Noble Truths instead of dependent origination.

The Four Noble Truths, dependent origination, and the three Dharma seals are the most basic principles of Buddhist doctrine. Though the three are different, they are all interrelated. The Four Noble Truths simply turn the focus of dependent origination directly onto human life. For this reason, they seem more relevant to human beings and easier to understand.

The Four Noble Truths are: the truth of suffering, the truth of the causes of suffering, the truth of the cessation of suffering, and the truth of the path leading to the cessation of suffering. The word "suffering" in this instance is a standard English translation of the Sanskrit word *duhkha*, which literally means "unsatisfactory."

THE SIGNIFICANCE OF THE FOUR NOBLE TRUTHS

In Chinese, the Four Noble Truths are called *si shengdi* (四聖諦). The character *sheng* (聖) means "correct" or "righteous." This is explained in the sutras as such, "The noble are also righteous, and they apply righteousness in all matters. This is why they are called 'noble.'"

The character *di* (諦) means "truth" and "examination" and is explained in the *Treatise on the Stages of Yogacara Practitioners* as such, "From the truth of suffering to the truth of the path leading to the cessation of suffering, all are true, and not inverted. That is why they are called 'truths.'" It also says, "Only those who are noble can understand these truths and contemplate them. Those who are ignorant can neither understand them nor contemplate them. Thus, these truths are called 'noble truths.'" When we can fully understand the Four Noble Truths, we are noble.

The *Commentary on the Treatise of the Middle Way* says, "The Four Noble Truths are the root of ignorance and awakening. In the state of ignorance, you will be trapped within the chaos of the six realms of existence. In the state of awakening, you will become a sage of the three vehicles."

The *Sutra of Teachings Bequeathed by the Buddha* says, "The moon may become hot and the sun may grow cold, but the Four Noble Truths will never change."

The Four Noble Truths stand at the core of all life. They explain all phenomena in the universe, and they teach us how to achieve liberation from all delusions.

Understanding the Four Noble Truths depends on wisdom. The first truth says that life is full of suffering. The second truth says that suffering is caused by our attachments. The third truth says that awakening or complete liberation from all suffering is possible. The fourth truth teaches us how to awaken.

The first two of the Four Noble Truths have a cause and effect relationship with each other. The first truth is the effect and the second is its cause. The third and fourth truths also have a cause and effect relationship with each other. The third truth is an effect that is caused by the fourth truth.

At first glance, you might wonder why the Buddha placed the Four Noble Truths in the order he did. It seems more logical to place the second and fourth truths, which are both causes, before the first and the third truths, which are both effects. The Buddha chose to use a different order because he wanted to teach them in the most effective way possible. Since it is easier for most people to grasp the effect and then come to understand its causes, the Buddha placed the truth of suffering first. Then he explained the causes of suffering. Once people understand the first two noble truths, they naturally want to liberate themselves from their suffering. To help us understand how to achieve liberation, the Buddha taught the third noble truth, which is the cessation of suffering. Then he taught the fourth noble truth, which is the path that leads to the cessation of suffering.

Central to all of the Buddha's teachings is the immense compassion he showed in crafting explanations that are designed to be understandable to everyone. Dependent origination and the Four Noble Truths are very profound truths, and as we learn more about them we can see how the Buddha's wisdom and compassion allowed him to teach them so clearly.

THE FIRST NOBLE TRUTH

Suffering is the state in which the body and mind are driven by afflictions. The truth of suffering describes how life is full of suffering. The Buddha saw with perfect clarity that each one of us cannot escape from this reality, and that it is not possible for a human being to achieve complete satisfaction in this world. Buddhist sutras show suffering in many different ways. In the following sections, I will discuss the three most basic classifications of suffering as described in the sutras.

The Two Kinds of Suffering

These are internal suffering and external suffering. This is the most basic classification of suffering mentioned in the Buddhist sutras, and is very easy to understand. Internal suffering is suffering that we usually think of as being part of ourselves. These include physical pain, anxiety, fear, jealousy, suspicion, anger, and so forth. External suffering is suffering that comes from the outside. These include wind, rain, cold, heat, drought, wild animals, natural disasters, wars, criminals, and all other manner of things. Both kinds of suffering, internal and external, are unavoidable.

The Three Kinds of Suffering

These focus more on the quality of suffering rather than on its origin or type. The first of the three is suffering within suffering, the suffering that comes from just being alive as well as the conditions of hunger, disease, wind and rain, labor, heat and cold, and casualties of war. The second is the suffering of loss. The suffering of loss refers to the loss of happiness. This is caused by the passage of time, or is broken down by external conditions leading to the suffering of the body and mind. For example, objects break, people die, and everything ages and declines. Even the best of times must all come to an end. The third suffering is the suffering of impermanence. The suffering of impermanence is that which comes from living in a world where everything is constantly changing. In our world, we have little or no control over our lives. We experience anxiety, fear, and helplessness as we watch everything change from day to day.

The Eight Kinds of Suffering

These are a more detailed description of the suffering that all sentient beings must endure. They are grouped according to their content.

The first is the suffering of birth. Following many dangerous months in our mother's womb, we at last experience the pain and fear of birth. After that, anything can happen. We are like prisoners in our bodies and of the worlds into which we are born.

The second is the suffering of old age. If we are fortunate enough not to die when we are still young, we will have to face the suffering of growing old and of watching our physical and mental qualities decline.

The third is the suffering of illness. When we are sick, we might suffer from aches and pains, cuts and bruises, poor digestion, organ failure, paralysis, or respiratory problems. All of us at some time must suffer from the pain of illness.

The fourth is the suffering of death. Even if our lives are somehow perfect, we will still die. If death is not sudden and frightening, then it is too often slow and painful. Especially at the moment of death, when the body and mind begin to decompose, there is extreme suffering. This is what is meant by the suffering of death.

The fifth is the suffering of separation from loved ones. It stems from our strong attachments. Sometimes we lose the ones we love, and sometimes they do not love us in return. We suffer because we cannot always be with the people we love.

The sixth is the suffering of closeness to loathsome people. When we have to deal with people we really dislike, we suffer. For example, at work we might dislike our boss, or we cannot tolerate a particular coworker. However, when we are forced to interact with them, we suffer.

The seventh is the suffering of not getting what we want. As human beings, we have attachments. When we encounter objects of our desire and we doggedly pursue them, but we still cannot obtain them, we suffer.

The eighth is the suffering of the five aggregates, which are the five components of existence: form, feeling, perception, mental formations, and consciousness. They are the "building blocks" of a sentient being, and the means through which all suffering occurs. When the five aggregates come together, they become the unlimited fuel source that produces pain and suffering, life after life.

The Basic Causes of Suffering

In the above sections, we have discussed some of the basic ways Buddhists understand human life as being mired in suffering. In the following sections, we will look more deeply into the subject of suffering as we delineate some of its most basic causes.

1. *The self is not in harmony with the material world.* We are constantly struggling to find comfort in this world. When our houses are too small and there are too many people,

we will feel uncomfortable. When our desk is too high or too low, the lamp is too bright or too dim, we may find it difficult to study with ease. The material world does not revolve around us in just the way we would like, so we suffer.

2. *The self is not in harmony with other people.* All too often we cannot be with the people we want to be with, but are forced to spend time with people who are difficult for us to get along with. Sometimes, we are even forced to spend time with people who openly dislike us.

3. *The self is not in harmony with the body.* The body is born, grows old, gets sick, and dies. The self has little or no control over this process.

4. *The self and the mind are not in harmony.* Our mind is often beyond our control. It races from one idea to the next like a wild horse. Delusional thought is the source of all of our suffering. Although we may know this, we still find it very hard to control the mind.

5. *The self and its desires are not in harmony.* There are good desires and bad desires. Good desires can improve the self, and even benefit others. However, if we poorly manage these desires, they may become burdens. Bad desires, such as coveting material things and being attached to physical desire, create even more suffering than when we mismanage our good desires. We may understand that desire produces karma and suffering, but that does not mean the

mind will be able to control itself easily. Self-control is difficult precisely because what we know to be best for us is not always what we most want. If we do not even bother to control our desires, but instead give them free rein, then the self will suffer even more.

6. *The self and its views are not in good harmony.* This basically means that we have wrong views or false perceptions. When what we believe is not in accordance with the truth, we cause ourselves endless trouble because we will be prone to repeat the same mistakes over and over again.

7. *The self is not in harmony with nature.* Rain, flood, droughts, storms, waves, and all of the other forces of nature are beyond our control and often can cause us to suffer.

The Buddha taught the truth of suffering not to make us despair but to help us clearly recognize the realities of life. When we understand the extent of our suffering and the impossibility of avoiding it, we should feel inspired to overcome it.

THE SECOND NOBLE TRUTH

The second noble truth is the truth of the causes of suffering. The origin of the causes of all suffering lie is our greed, anger, and ignorance, also known as the three poisons. Sentient beings chain themselves to the painful and delusive world through their strong attachments to these three poisons.

THE THIRD NOBLE TRUTH

The third noble truth is the truth of the cessation of suffering. "Cessation of suffering" is another term for *nirvana*, a state that cannot be described by language. It is beyond greed, anger, ignorance, and suffering. *Nirvana* is also beyond all duality and all distinctions between right and wrong, self and other, good and bad, and birth and death.

THE FOURTH NOBLE TRUTH

The fourth noble truth is the truth of the path leading to the cessation of suffering. The Way to the cessation of suffering is the path that shows us how to overcome the causes of suffering and leads to *nirvana*. The most basic way to overcome the causes of suffering is to follow the Noble Eightfold Path.

THE IMPORTANCE OF THE FOUR NOBLE TRUTHS

The Four Noble Truths were the first teachings of the Buddha, and they were among his last teachings. When he neared his death, the Buddha told his disciples that if any of them had any doubt about the validity of the Four Noble Truths, they should speak up and have their questions answered before it was too late. The close attention that the Buddha paid to the Four Noble Truths throughout his forty-nine years of teaching shows the importance he placed on them.

When the Buddha was teaching the Four Noble Truths, he explained it three times from three different angles in order to help us better understand his message. These three explanations are called the "three turnings of the Dharma wheel of the Four Noble Truths."

The first turning of the Dharma wheel was instructive. The Buddha explained the content and meaning of the Four Noble Truths to his disciples so that they might understand their importance. He said, "Such is suffering, which is oppressive. Such is the cause of suffering, which beckons. Such is the cessation of suffering, which is attainable. Such is the path, which can be practiced."

The second turning of the Dharma wheel was to provide encouragement. In this assembly, the Buddha taught the methods for cultivating the Four Noble Truths and encouraged his disciples to practice these methods in order to sever their afflictions and attain liberation. The Buddha said, "Such is suffering, you should understand it. Such is the cause of suffering, you should end it. Such is the cessation of suffering, you should realize it. Such is the path, you should practice it."

In the third turning of the Dharma wheel the Buddha shared his realization. Here, the Buddha showed his disciples that he had already realized the Four Noble Truths, and encouraged them to diligently practice so that they too could realize these truths. He said, "Such is suffering, I have understood it. Such is the cause of suffering, I have ended it. Such is the cessation of suffering, I have realized it. Such is the path; I have practiced it."

The Buddha is sometimes called the "Great Doctor" because his teachings can cure us of the disease of our attachments. The best way to end suffering is to understand the Four Noble Truths. If the Four Noble Truths are properly understood, the rest of the Buddha's teachings become much easier to understand. If the Buddha's teachings are understood and practiced, they can lead to liberation from all suffering and pain. The Buddha is the doctor and he has the medicine; all we need to do is take it.

Chapter Five

KARMA

Karma is a Sanskrit word that means "action" or "deed." It is
the universal law that governs the cause and effect of intentional deeds, and states that all intentional deeds produce results
that eventually will be felt by the doer of the deed. Good deeds
produce positive karmic effects and bad deeds produce negative
karmic effects. Karma operates at many levels. Individuals have
karma, communities have karma, countries have karma, and the
earth as a whole has karma.

When we say that a person "has" karma, we mean that person's
present life is conditioned by his previous behavior. The same can
be said of groups of people, countries, and the earth we inhabit.

The concept of karma is central to all schools of Buddhism
and all interpretations of the Dharma. No one could possibly understand Buddhism without fully understanding the concept of
karma. The Buddha divided karma into three types: karma generated by the body, karma generated by speech, and karma generated
by the mind. All intentional acts of body, speech, and mind will

inevitably produce karmic results. Even a Buddha cannot change the results of karma.

For most people, karma works through repetition. A certain intentional act produces a certain karmic result. Then this result is reacted to, and this reaction leads to another karmic result, and so on and so forth. Our lives are built upon our own reactions to conditions we have created ourselves. By reacting to our own karma over and over again, we mire ourselves in delusion. The Buddha said that the cycle of birth and death is a delusion that we cling to because we are not able to see beyond it. He said that we do not understand how to escape the cycle because we do not understand how it works. More than anything else, it is karma that keeps sentient beings trapped in the cycle of birth and death. However, if karma is truly understood, sentient beings can be liberated from this cycle.

For the purpose of this discussion, "negative karma" is generated from actions that harm sentient beings while "positive karma" is generated by actions which help them. Positive karma leads to rebirth as a human being or a heavenly being. On the other hand, negative karma is any action that harms and causes suffering to self or others. Very harmful acts produce negative karma that leads to rebirth in one of the three lower realms of existence (the realms of hell, hungry ghosts, and animals).

Karma is the force that causes us to be born even if we do not want to be born and causes us to die even if we do not want to die. However, it is important to understand that in the cycle of birth and death it is not "we" who are being born again and again, but rather it is our karma. Buddhist practice places great emphasis on doing good deeds because the good that we do today will form the foundation for future lives. The right way to understand karma is not to think about what we are going to "get out of" our actions, but rather to pay attention to what we doing right now, and what the effects of our actions will be.

THE DIFFERENT KINDS OF KARMA

Generally speaking, karma is divided into three basic kinds: the karma of body, speech, and mind. Whenever we form an intention, we have planted a mental karmic seed. As soon as we act on that intention, we have added more seeds to that first seed.

Positive Karma, Negative Karma, and Neutral Karma

Some acts produce positive karma, some produce negative karma, and some produce neutral karma. Positive karma is produced by acts that are intended to help other sentient beings. This includes protecting animals, giving to charity, speaking kind and encouraging words, and thinking compassionate thoughts. Negative karma is produced by acts that are intended to harm oneself or others. For example, killing, stealing, sexual misconduct, lying, speaking harsh words, anger, greed, and wrong views all create negative karma. Unintentional acts produce neutral karma, which are actions that have no good or bad consequence. These actions also include involuntary behaviors like sleeping, walking, breathing, and eating.

Guiding Karma and Complete Karma

Guiding karma, also called "general karma," are those karmic effects which guide the realm of existence a sentient being is reborn in: in the human realm, the animal realm, the hungry ghost realm, and so forth. Complete karma, also called "specific karma," are those karmic effects which complete the other attributes of a being's life, such as physical appearance, personality, health, lifespan, and external circumstances like which family and nation one will be born into.

Collective Karma and Individual Karma

Collective karma is a karmic effect that is shared by many different beings at once. For example, human beings are born on this earth because they have the same karmic causes, and therefore, share the same result. The nation and region in which we live is also part of our collective karma. If our region experiences a flood or an earthquake, it too is a karmic result we share with the people who live in our area.

The extent to which different collective karmic effects are shared among people varies. When an earthquake strikes an area, everyone in that area is affected in some way by the earthquake. This is collective karma that is shared by all. However, each individual in that area will be affected by the earthquake differently. Some may be injured, some will not. Some may lose their homes, while others experience no damage at all. This is the kind of collective karma that is not shared by all. The same distinction could be made for a car accident or any other event that affects more than one person. In the same car accident, one person may be killed whereas another walks away unharmed.

People also have individual karma that is different from person to person. Even if several people are involved in the same situation, they may have different reactions to it. For example, each member of a family has different individual karma, but when there is an event like a death in the family all members of the family will feel pain and grief. But when two strangers meet on the street, they are involved in the same situation, but their reaction to one another may be very different.

Definite Karma and Indefinite Karma

Definite karma is karma that will produce an effect at a determined time and place, and cannot be avoided by any means. Indefinite karma is karma that has an indefinite result. This is because the right conditions have not yet ripened, so the time, place, and means of the result have not been determined.

The Four Types of Karma

Another way to understand our actions is to divide them into four different types based on the karmic effects they produce: negative karma, positive karma, both negative and positive karma, and neither negative or positive karma. "Negative karma" are those actions which will only produce negative karmic effects, and "positive karma" are those actions which will only produce positive karmic effects. Those actions which are both negative and positive karma produce some negative karmic effects, and some positive karmic effects. Neither negative nor positive karma is also called "karma without outflows," and is the karma of awakened beings who have severed all defilements and attained liberation. Since they have transcended the duality of good and bad, positive and negative, they no longer produce either positive karma or negative karma.

THE ORDER IN WHICH KARMA ARRIVES

Karmic relationships are very complex and difficult to understand, and yet karmic effects arrive in a definite order. An understanding of this order is important to strengthen one's faith in karma.

Without understanding the order in which karmic effects arrive, it is too easy to see good people suffering hard deaths, bad people enjoying easy lives, and conclude that there is no justice in the world and no such thing as karma.

In terms of order, karmic effects arrive at three different times: causes in this life which manifest as effects in this life, causes in this life which manifest as effects in the next life, and causes in this life which manifest as effects in some future life beyond the next. These three levels can be compared to different kinds of plants: some seeds planted in the spring can be harvested in the fall, while others may take a whole year to bear fruit. Other trees may not bear fruit for several years.

Karmic effects arrive at different times for two main reasons. First, the karmic cause may generate an effect either slowly or quickly. This is similar to the plants that may be harvested in a single season or in a number of years as stated above. Another reason is that the necessary conditions may either be present or not present. For example, even if a seed is of the type that grows quickly, if it is not watered and kept in the dark it may not grow for many years.

That is why good people may still suffer: the negative karma from previous lifetimes has ripened in the present lifetime. Although they might have performed good deeds in this lifetime, the karmic causes of those good deeds are slow and the right conditions are not yet present, so the karmic effects will not appear until future lifetimes. By the same principle, people who do bad things may still lead comfortable lives. The seeds they are planting today will bring them misery in the future, but before that day comes, they are receiving the results of good deeds done in past lives.

There are two important points concerning the inner working of karma that are important to explain. First, karmic causes do not disappear, and second, negative karma and positive karma do not "cancel each other out." The only way to avoid a negative effect is not to generate a negative cause. As long as we create a karmic cause it will reside in our consciousness until the right conditions are present and then manifest as an effect.

Also, while negative karma and positive karma do not cancel each other out, the more good deeds we perform our negative karma will manifest as less severe effects, and our positive karma will ripen more quickly. This is like adding fresh water to a glass of salt water: the salt has not been removed, but the taste is much less salty.

There are three factors which contribute to which realm we will be reborn in when our lives come to an end: the weightiness of our positive and negative karma, our habitual tendencies, and our final recollection. At the end of our life, counting all of the positive and negative karma we have accumulated, either our positive karma or negative karma will weigh more heavily on our future rebirth, depending on the frequency and severity of our good and bad deeds. Likewise, our habitual tendencies, our patterns of behavior that we generate in life, contribute to our future rebirth. Lastly, our final recollection, the thoughts we generate in our final moments of life, contribute to our future rebirth. Consider going for a walk around the neighborhood: you may not have any particular goal, but when you arrive at an intersection you must still choose whether to go north, south, east, or west. Suppose you then have a thought that you have a friend who lives on the west side, so you choose to go west. Just as a single thought affects our choice of direction, our thoughts before death, whether wholesome or unwholesome, have a profound effect on our future rebirth.

PRINCIPLES OF KARMA

The Buddha said that all phenomena are impermanent. If all things are changing moment by moment, and if nothing is eternal, why does karma continue from life to life? In the Buddhist sutras, karma is commonly compared to seeds. A seed may be stored for many years, but as soon as it meets the right conditions, it will begin to sprout, then grow, bloom, and bear fruit. Over time, its flowers will produce more seeds. And these seeds, after meeting with the right conditions, will grow again. Karma works in the same way, for all of our intentional acts produce "seeds" that are stored in our consciousness. When the conditions are right, those karmic causes will manifest as effects.

Karma is also our persistent traits or attributes from one life to the next. Our karma is like the fragrance that persists in the bottle even after the perfume has been used up. The habitual tendencies and karma of one life will persist into the next life in a similar way. Once a karmic cause has been "planted," it cannot be destroyed. The effect that will manifest is a direct reflection of the karmic cause, and the person who created the karmic cause must alone bear the effect of its fruition.

All sentient beings are trapped in the ocean of birth and death due to their karma. Karma is like the string that holds prayer beads together. The string connects all the beads; likewise, karma connects our lives from the past to the present and into the future, continuously causing us to be reborn in the six realms of existence. Therefore, our physical bodies are born and die, but life does not end. When we break a teacup, the pieces of the cup cannot be put back together. However, the contents inside the cup do not diminish even when they flow onto the table and then to the ground.

Karma is like the tea that does not disappear; rather, it continues to exist in another incarnation. In this cycle, each person must bear his or her own positive and negative karma. Gods and spirits are not here to either reward or punish us.

Since karma is created by each person and not controlled by the gods, everyone is equal under the law of karma. In fact, karma should bring us hope. Doing good deeds is like depositing money in the bank. If we do not keep on saving, there will come a day when our money is all used up. Therefore, we need to continue to generate positive karma by performing good deeds. Conversely, if we commit many bad deeds, it is like being heavily in debt. But, if we change our ways and start performing good deeds, one day we will be able to pay back what we owe.

Karma lets us understand why all sentient beings are reborn into the cycle of brth and death, and how they are related to each other. Knowing this can give rise to great compassion. By having great compassion and living in accord with karma not only can we be happy in this life, but be reborn into a higher realm in the next life.

Chapter Six

THE THREE DHARMA SEALS

B uddhists say that for something to be true it must have the following basic characteristics: it must be universally true and apply to all things equally, it must be certainly true and happen every time, it must be true in the past, present, and future.

For example, all people are born and all people must die. This is an ultimate truth because it is true not just for Chinese, Indians, Australians, or Americans, but for all people at all times. Birth and death are universal and certain, and occur in the past, present, and future.

The "three Dharma seals" are truths that affirm the Dharma and are common to all Buddhist traditions. They possess all four qualities mentioned above, and they can be proven both through reasoning and observation. They are also the means by which to judge whether or not something is truly the Dharma: teachings which accord with the three Dharma seals are true, and those which do not are false. The three Dharma seals are:

1. All conditioned phenomena are impermanent.
2. All phenomena are without an independent self.
3. *Nirvana* is perfect tranquility.

Impermanence, lack of an independent self, and *nirvana* are called the Dharma "seals" because all phenomena are "stamped" with them. There is nothing that does not possess these three characteristics. Another reason that Buddhists call these three truths "Dharma seals" is that they are similar to official seals that prove documents are real and not forged. If any so-called "truth" contradicts the three Dharma seals, then it cannot be an authentic teaching of the Buddha. When a teaching is not stamped by the three Dharma seals, it cannot be true. If something is supposedly said by the Buddha himself, but contradicts the three Dharma seals, it cannot be true. In this same vein, any truth that is stamped with all of the three Dharma seals must be true, whether a Buddha said it or not. These principles are so fundamental to Buddhism that it can further be said that any truth that is stamped with the three Dharma seals is rightfully part of the Dharma.

THE FIRST DHARMA SEAL

The first Dharma seal says that all conditioned phenomena are impermanent. This means that all phenomena change; nothing can forever stay the same. All phenomena are constantly interacting with each other, constantly influencing each other, and constantly causing each other to change. In the constant flow of time from past, present, to future, all phenomena are changing from one instant to the next. Within each moment, they arise and cease.

All things change. Sentient beings are born, grow old, get sick, and die. The environment changes from season to season and year to year. Stars form, exist, and die. Thoughts arise, abide, change, and cease. Everything is like this: every moment, the phenomenal world is moving between the four states of birth, abiding, decay, and death. Nothing is permanent.

According to Buddhist sutras, there are two basic kinds of impermanence: momentary impermanence and periodic impermanence.

Momentary Impermanence

In Buddhism, a *ksana* is the smallest possible moment of time. Within the context of how we measure time today, it is approximately one seventy-fifth of a second. The *Record of Investigations of Mysteries* states, "A *ksana* is a 'moment' of thought. A single snap of the fingers contains sixty *ksana*." Among all phenomena, those that change most quickly are our thoughts.

According to the *Treatise on the Great Compendium of the Abhidharma*, "In one day, there are 6,400,099,980 *ksanas* worth of the five aggregates arising and extinguishing." The *Rain of Treasures Sutra* says, "The deluded mind is like running water; it rises and falls without stopping. Like lightning, the moments come and go and do not remain."

The thoughts in our mind are constantly changing from one moment to the next. Material things change as well, from when they are new until they have become old, but they do not change suddenly. Rather, these changes are constantly occurring from one moment to the next. This is why we say it is momentary impermanence.

Periodic Impermanence

Since all phenomena are in a constant state of change, over a long period of time, they will be extinguished. This process is called "periodic impermanence," and is really just an accumulation of episodes of momentary impermanence mentioned above. The processes of birth, aging, sickness, and death in sentient beings; the processes of arising, abiding, changing, and ceasing in phenomena; and the process of formation, abiding, decay, and emptiness in the universe itself are all built out of moments of gradual change. When these gradual changes accumulate, substantial changes can be observed.

Understanding the first Dharma seal is important because once we recognize the brevity of life and the impermanence of all things, we will be motivated to delve even deeper into the truths of Buddhism. Impermanence should not frighten. Rather, it should inspire us to appreciate our time on earth. We should understand that as difficult as life may be, we should always try to live a good life.

The *Mahaparinirvana Sutra* says, "All phenomena are impermanent. Loved ones who come together must one day separate." Recognizing the impermanence of all things can inspire us to help all sentient beings realize the Buddha nature within.

THE SECOND DHARMA SEAL

Not only are all phenomena impermanent, but they are also devoid of an "independent self." Not having an independent self nature means that all phenomena depend upon other things for their existence, and would not be able to exist without them. The word "phenomena" in this case refers to all tangible and intangible things, all events, all thoughts, all laws, and everything else.

To say that nothing has a self is to say that nothing has any attribute that endures over long periods of time. There is no "self" that always stays the same. If the "self" cannot possibly stay the same, then how can it really be a self?

The second Dharma seal goes right to the heart of human psychology. You may say that you do not believe that anything has a self, but chances are you will act and think as if you do. Our thought patterns generally gravitate toward absolutes: things are the way they are, they have always been that way, and they will stay that way. Solid things seem permanent to us. Our sense of self seems immutable. We think, "I am who I am, and I will stay that way."

The truth is that we are always changing, just as everything else is always changing. Not only do things not have a self, but neither do we. Most of the world's religions maintain the exact opposite. They claim that an absolute, eternal, and completely perfect god created human beings and their eternal souls.

Buddhism denies "self" in two basic ways. First, it states that sentient beings are without "self." Most people are very attached to their bodies and this attachment leads them to believe that there is some absolute essence inside of them that is the "real" self. The Buddha said that the body is formed by the five aggregates and the accumulation of karma. It is a temporary form caused by a brief congregation of the physical and mental components of existence. Just as a house is made up of many parts, the body is also made of many components that create a substantial existence. Once those parts are separated, no real self will be found anywhere.

Second, Buddhism teaches that all phenomena are without self. Phenomena arise due to other phenomena. When the causes and conditions that produce and uphold them are removed, all phenomena cease to be. To say that phenomena have no self is another way of saying that their existence is dependent on one another. It is important to understand these basic ideas because they are fundamental to all Buddhist practice.

THE THIRD DHARMA SEAL

Nirvana is the third noble truth: the cessation of suffering. According to the *Commentary on the Flower Adornment Sutra*, "*Nirvana* means cessation." The *Mahaparinirvana Sutra* also says, "The cessation of all suffering is *nirvana*." Since suffering is caused by delusion, *nirvana* is the cessation of delusion; since suffering is caused by the belief in duality, *nirvana* is the cessation of duality. *Nirvana* is also the cessation of the belief in an independent self and the cessation of the birth and death of that "self." Because there is no more suffering, *nirvana* is the state of perfect tranquility.

When we say *nirvana* is the state of perfect tranquility, it refers to the state in which greed, anger, ignorance, arrogance, and doubt are eliminated. It is the state in which the body does not commit unwholesome deeds and the mind does not have unwholesome thoughts. It is a state of liberation.

Buddhists generally understand four varieties of *nirvana*: pure *nirvana* of inherent nature, *nirvana* with remainder, *nirvana* without remainder, and non-abiding *nirvana*.

Nirvana of intrinsic nature is also called "intrinsically pure *nirvana*." It is another word for Buddha nature, the intrinsically pure nature of all things. When the Buddha first awakened under the bodhi tree he exclaimed, "Marvelous, marvelous! All sentient beings have the Buddha's wisdom and virtue, but they fail to realize it because they cling to deluded thoughts and attachments."

Nirvana with remainder describes the state of an awakened being who still has a physical body. "With remainder" means that the past karma associated with the body still remains. An awakened being is liberated from all defilements of the mind and creates no new karma, but his physical body is still subject to the karmic effects from the past.

Nirvana without remainder describes the state of an awakened being when the physical body no longer remains. The awakened being will never again be subject to the cycle of birth and death.

Nirvana without abiding is the fourth classification of *nirvana,* and describes the *nirvana* of Buddhas and bodhisattvas. A great bodhisattva has great wisdom and has severed all defilements, and as such they do not abide in our world. However, because of great compassion for all sentient beings, they choose not to enter the state of perfect tranquility. This state of not dwelling in our world and not entering perfect tranquility is known as *nirvana* without abiding.

The Buddhist sutras describe *nirvana* with many other names. One common one is the Sanskrit term *anuttara samyak sambodhi,* "complete, perfect, unsurpassed awakening." *Nirvana* is also commonly called "attaining the Dharma body." This term has many meanings, but it refers to the aspect of the Buddha which is manifest throughout the universe. The *Lion's Roar of Queen Srimala Sutra* says, "The Dharma body is the great *nirvana*-body of the Buddha."

Nirvana is also called the "Dharma realm of all Buddhas." It is also called the "deepest *samadhi,*" meaning the greatest level of meditative concentration. *Nirvana* is a state of blissful purity that only a Buddha has fully attained. The *Lotus Sutra* says, "Only the Buddha has attained great awakening. This state of complete and perfect wisdom is called great *nirvana.*"

Sakyamuni Buddha taught the three Dharma seals to help us eliminate our defilements. Contemplation of the three Dharma seals helps us overcome delusion because the three Dharma seals cut off delusion at its three primary points. They teach us to understand that all phenomena are impermanent and devoid of an independent existence. At the same time they teach us that contemplating these truths should not lead us to despair because all sentient beings possess Buddha nature. In the *Lotus Sutra*, the Buddha says, "I speak of the three Dharma seals to benefit all sentient beings in the world."

UNDERSTANDING THE THREE DHARMA SEALS

People sometimes think that Buddhism is a pessimistic religion because it talks so much about emptiness, impermanence, and suffering. The Buddha spoke of these basic truths not because he was pessimistic but because he wanted people to fully understand delusion. The Buddha knew that once delusion is understood, it loses its powerful hold over us. Once we see delusion for what it is, we will want to be rid of it so we can be more aware of things as they are. The three Dharma seals should not make us feel despair, but instead be what allows us to transcend despair.

Hopeful Impermanence

Most people instinctively react negatively to the first Dharma seal, because they think that impermanence only means that what is good will get worse. While this may be true in some cases, it is just as true that what is bad can get better. Impermanence is a great source of hope, for it teaches us that as hard as our present circumstances may be, they can change. If we have diligently cultivated good karmic causes, then the changes will inevitably be changes for the better.

Properly understood, the concept of impermanence can be a great aid in difficult situations. If we are poor, impermanence can teach us that our circumstances will not last forever. If we meet with a setback in our work, it can teach us not to despair. If we meet with hardship or tragedy, impermanence can teach us that one day, things will change again for the better. Impermanence tells us that nothing stays the same; it teaches us that things can change for the better if we truly work to better our circumstances.

Contemplating impermanence also helps us to treasure what we have. Impermanence teaches us to be grateful for every moment of life and to use our time as productively as we can. It reminds us that if we do not make progress in Buddhism now, we may have to wait many lifetimes before we encounter the Dharma again. Impermanence inspires us to progress, study, and learn. Now is the time to act, because the present is all the time that we really have.

No-Self Teaches Us How to Cooperate

The reason Buddhists emphasize the lack of an independent self is to help each one of us get past the narcissistic devotion we normally feel toward our body and the deluded belief that the body "proves" that there is some absolute "self." Attachment to the self is the root source of all delusion. It produces anger and greed, and keeps us bound firmly to ignorance. Contemplation of the second Dharma seal will teach us how to break the bonds of self-love.

The human body is produced by conditions, and it is made up of physical and mental components. When conditions bring those components together, a body is formed. When those same conditions disperse, the body will cease to be. There is no substantial existence or absolute self present anywhere in the body.

From the time we are born to the time we die, all of us change all of the time. There is nothing eternal or permanent about us. Knowing this can be a great help if we find ourselves trapped in adverse circumstances. Contemplation of no-self can remove deep-seated and painful feelings that arise from the erroneous belief that we possess a permanent self that really can be threatened, or insulted, or defamed. The *Great Stopping and Seeing* says, "When there is no wisdom, we will perceive the self as real. When we contemplate with wisdom, the self will be recognized as unreal."

In understanding the concept of non-self, it is important not to fall into the mistaken belief that you as a person are not here or that you do not exist. Most Buddhist beliefs and ideas should be understood on at least two different levels. One level is called the "mundane level," and has to do with how things appear from an ordinary, worldly perspective. But there is also the "supramundane level," which is concerned with the absolute and transcendent nature of reality.

Mundane truths are important, because they help us to understand the world we all live in. We must all learn to function with the mundane understanding of "self," because it is a concept upon which our languages and society are built.

The second Dharma seal is a teaching which operates at the supramundane level. This type of understanding is not entirely separate from the world in which we live, because once we understand that our mundane assumptions about the world are based on observations of temporary existence our ability to function in the world will be greatly enhanced. The truth of non-self should be used when it can help us understand life, but it should not become a prism that is used to distort life or an excuse to avoid life.

When the second Dharma seal is understood, it allows us to more fully participate in life, because it provides a basis for us to cooperate with other sentient beings. Knowing that all phenomena lack an independent self teaches us to get along with others because it clearly shows that we are sustained by many conditions, and others are too. In the same way that we need others, they need us too.

Buddhism places great emphasis on the welfare of all sentient beings. The Buddha spent forty-nine years teaching the Dharma, so none of us should believe that the truth of non-self is a reason to abandon other beings for a life of complete seclusion. On the contrary, the second Dharma seal is a reason to become involved in the community and live among other sentient beings. When we see others as ourselves and ourselves as part of a much larger whole, then, and only then, will we have fully understood the second Dharma seal.

Nirvana Is the Ultimate Refuge

Most people believe that *nirvana* is attained only after death. Actually, *nirvana* is beyond birth and death. It is the state where the attachment to self and phenomena is extinguished, the state where all afflictions and defilements are eliminated, and the state of liberation from the cycle of birth and death.

In the same way that a criminal loses his freedom by being shackled and manacled, so too are sentient beings bound by the chains of greed, hatred, and ignorance. The Dharma can liberate us from these defilements, and allow us to attain *nirvana*.

Life is like a turbulent ocean, with crashing waves coming one after another. The continuous movement of the ocean exemplifies the impermanence of all phenomena. But, if we can look at the waves through the eyes of the Buddhist sages, we can see that although the waves are turbulent, the nature of water is to be calm. Likewise, life is an endless cycle of birth and death, but our intrinsic nature is a state of perfect peace. Thus, if we want to attain the liberation and tranquility of *nirvana*, we must realize it in the impermanence and non-self of all phenomena.

To be in *nirvana* is to be beyond all time and space, all duality, all delusion, and all fear. *Nirvana* is the ultimate refuge of all life. To understand the third Dharma seal is to understand that *nirvana* is the pure Buddha mind, the truth that lies at the center of all of the Buddha's teachings. One does not need to wait for death to experience *nirvana* because *nirvana* is always present in everything.

Chapter Seven

EMPTINESS

Buddhism has been called the "teaching of emptiness" since ancient times because emptiness is one of its most important doctrines. Emptiness is also one of the characteristics that distinguishes Buddhism from other religions.

As previously mentioned, when the Buddha attained awakening under the bodhi tree, he awakened to the universal truth of dependent origination. Dependent origination means that everything in the world arises from causes and conditions, and that nothing has an independent self. The characteristic of all phenomena having no independent self is called "emptiness."

The word "emptiness" is an English translation of the Sanskrit word *sunyata* or the Chinese character *kong* (空). In Buddhist terminology, emptiness is used to describe the ultimate nature of reality. However, emptiness is often misinterpreted and instead seen as a justification for pessimism and seclusion. When understood correctly, one will see that emptiness embraces the boundless universe and gives rise to all existence. Emptiness is not negation;

it is emptying the mind of the notions of relativity, duality, and distinction. Emptiness is even letting go of our attachment to emptiness itself. With a mind such as this, we will attain the state of ease and liberation, a state with no duality between emptiness and existence.

THE TRUE MEANING OF EMPTINESS

The *Treatise on the Middle Way* says, "Because there is emptiness, all phenomena exist. Without emptiness, all phenomena could not be." Without emptiness, the phenomenal world could not exist. For example, from the perspective of dependent origination, a piece of cotton cloth is "empty." Why? The cloth only exists temporarily, for it is conditioned by other things. The cloth is made from cotton yarn, and the yarn is made from cotton fiber. Cotton fiber comes from cottonseeds, and the seeds need soil, air, sunlight, water, and nutrients before they can grow into plants that produce cotton. Therefore, the cotton cloth is the result of the combination of many conditions that span the universe. Looking at all things from this point of view, we can see that the cloth's nature is empty. This core of emptiness is what allows all phenomena to exist.

Emptiness is a truth that connects the three Dharma seals. For example, nothing in the world is permanent and everything is always changing. This is the first Dharma seal, "all conditioned phenomena are impermanent." Even the nature of suffering is impermanent. According to the second Dharma seal, "all phenomena are without an independent self," such that everything relies upon many other things for its existence. No conditioned phenomena in the world is truly concrete, or truly tranquil—everything is like a dream, an illusion, a bubble, or a shadow. The exception is the third

Dharma seal, "*nirvana* is perfect tranquility," which the Buddha taught to help sentient beings achieve liberation. It demonstrates how true emptiness manifests wondrous existence.

Emptiness is an essential part of a wonderful and profound philosophy, but it is impossible to convey the meaning of emptiness in a single sentence. The *Explanation of the Treatise on the Awakening of Faith in Mahayana* lists ten different definitions for emptiness, and even though none of the ten definitions nor any definition can describe emptiness fully, these ten definitions can help to point us in the right direction:

1. Emptiness obstructs nothing. It pervades everything but obstructs nothing.
2. Emptiness embraces all places. It spreads everywhere and there is nowhere it is not present.
3. Emptiness is equality. It has no preference for one thing over another.
4. Emptiness is immense. It is vast, without limits and boundaries.
5. Emptiness is formless, it has no shape or form.
6. Emptiness is pure, and is without defilement.
7. Emptiness is motionless. It is always still. It is not born and does not die, and does not arise nor cease.
8. Emptiness is unlimited. It completely negates all things that have limits.
9. Emptiness is empty. It completely negates the substantial existence of all things and destroys all attachments to it.
10. Emptiness cannot be clung to, caught, or held.

DIFFERENT KINDS OF EMPTINESS

In Buddhist literature, many kinds of emptiness are discussed. However, emptiness can be classified into three basic kinds.

First, there is emptiness of the self, which is also known as emptiness of sentient beings. Since the life of all sentient beings is interconnected and dependent on causes and conditions, no single part of it can be said to have an independent existence in and of itself.

Second, there is the emptiness of all phenomena. In the same way as stated above, all phenomena are the result of causes and conditions, and thus have no independent existence. These phenomena also lack a "self."

Third, there is supreme emptiness. This is the emptiness that is beyond the duality of existence and non-existence, and does not abide in either. Supreme emptiness is also called the emptiness of "suchness," meaning the quality of things simply as they are. This type of emptiness is the same as the perfect tranquility of *nirvana*.

The *Treatise on the Perfection of Great Wisdom* says, "In the state of *nirvana*, there is no form of nirvana. The emptiness of *nirvana* is supreme emptiness... It leads all phenomena to the 'emptiness of suchness,' and is therefore called supreme emptiness."

HOW TO RECOGNIZE EMPTINESS

Emptiness and existence may seem like opposing concepts: existence seems as if it is anything other than empty, and emptiness seems as though it does not exist. However, from a Buddhist perspective, emptiness and existence are two sides of the same coin:

all of existence is empty because it lacks an independent self, but all of existence also arises out of emptiness itself.

How can we come to know emptiness? We can actually recognize emptiness from observing existence. The following are seven such approaches:

1. Continuous Succession

Nothing in the world is permanent or unchanging, and as all things fade away they will be replaced by what comes after. The cells of our bodies are an example of this: as cells divide, age, and die, they are replaced by new cells. Everything in the world is like this. There is an old Chinese saying that illustrates this continuous succession quite well, "In the Yangzi River, the waves from the back push the waves in front forward; just as a new generation of people replaces the old." By observing this continuous succession and impermanence of phenomena, we can understand emptiness.

2. Cycles

Everything in the universe is subject to cause and effect, which often manifests in the form of natural cycles. Consider the example of a fruit seed. If the seed is properly planted in the earth and receives sufficient sunlight, air, water, and other nutrients, it will grow into a plant, produce flowers, and then bear fruit. The seed is the cause, and the fruit is the effect. When the seed from this fruit is exposed to the necessary external conditions and once again grows into a plant bearing fruit, the fruit that was originally the effect becomes the cause of a new life. Causes lead to effects, and effects become causes. By observing these cycles we can understand emptiness.

3. Compounding of Elements

All phenomena are formed through the union of causes and conditions. For example, our body is composed of flesh, blood, sinew, and many other parts. If we separate all the constituent parts, the human body would no longer exist. By seeing how different components combine and come together we can understand emptiness.

4. Relative Existence

All things are defined by their relationship to other things. For example, in a three-story building, when a person walks from the first floor to the second floor, the second floor is "upstairs," the first floor is "downstairs." When that person walks from the third floor to the second floor, the second floor now becomes "downstairs." What is "upstairs" and "downstairs," "above" and "below" is not absolute. All things exist only in relation to one another. This is another way to understand emptiness.

5. No Absolute Standards

No phenomena has any "absolute standard" to which it can be compared. For example, consider light. Light can be produced from many sources: from a candle, from a gas lamp, or from an electric lamp, but there is no absolute standard for brightness. If we light a candle in the dark, we may consider the light from the candle to be bright. Yet, compared to the light from a lamp, the candlelight is no longer so bright. "Brightness" thus has no absolute standard. Observing the lack of absolute standards can help us to understand emptiness.

6. Temporary Names

Any given worldly phenomena has many different names or labels. Consider for a moment a piece of cloth: if it is worn over the upper body, we call it a shirt. If it is worn over the legs, we call it a skirt or a pair of pants. If it is worn over the feet, we call it socks, and if it is worn on the head, we call it a hat. In any instance, it is still a piece of cloth, but it is called by different names. When we see that each of these names is temporary, it can help us to understand emptiness.

7. Different Perspectives

Perception is not fixed, and is easily altered by our differing perspectives. On a snowy evening, a poet sitting by the window may be inspired by the beauty of the scene. He exclaims, "If it snows a few more feet, it will be even more beautiful!" At the same time, a homeless person huddled and shivering under an awning may lament, "If it snows a few more feet, how will I be able to make it through the night?" Although they face the same scene, due to their difference in perspectives, they have different perceptions. Seeing how much our perspectives affect our perceptions can help us to understand emptiness.

EMPTINESS AND EXISTENCE

The *Mahayana Esoteric Adornment Sutra* says, "Without emptiness, there is no form. Without form, there is no emptiness. The two are like the moon and moonlight: from beginning to end, they are always together." It is only because phenomena are empty that they can manifest, and it is only because they are impermanent that they reveal their empty nature. Existence could not be outside of emptiness, and emptiness is not truly empty outside of existence. Emptiness and existence always work hand in hand.

The teaching of emptiness is like an X-ray. With an X-ray, we can see into the hidden depths of the body. Through the truth of emptiness, we can see into the reality of all phenomena.

Emptiness is like the digit zero. The nature of zero is nothingness, but if we place a zero after a one, we get ten. If we add another zero, we get one hundred, and another gives us one thousand. From this, we can see that although zero may seem useless, it can become very useful. Emptiness is the same. Although some may say that emptiness is nothingness, emptiness can embrace everything in the universe.

We can experience emptiness in our everyday lives. For example, a "baby girl" gradually grows up and is called a "little girl." When she gets into her teens, she is known as a "young woman." After she reaches her twenties or thirties, she is called a "Miss," and if she marries, she is known as "Mrs. So-and-so." Having children, she becomes a "mother." When her children grow up and get married, she will gain more roles such as "mother-in-law" and even "grandmother." From the shift and changes in these titles, we can understand the truth of emptiness.

Beautiful and ugly, old and young, big and small are all relative terms and have no absolute standards. They are but temporary labels. The *Diamond Sutra* says, "There is no standard Dharma." It also says, "True reality is not reality." Only emptiness describes things as they are, for it is the unchanging Dharma. Only when we realize emptiness, will we truly understand the world. By understanding emptiness we can transcend duality and enter a world that is more open and profound.

Many may hear the Buddhist teaching on emptiness and think that it is negative, or that it encourages us to get rid of everything. In fact, the Buddhist concept of emptiness is not negative at all. On the contrary, emptiness is the basis of the arising of all existence. It is not a void, it is creation. Without an empty plot, we would not be able to build a house. If a bag were not empty, it could not contain anything. Without emptiness in the universe, human beings would not be able to survive. Hence, there must be emptiness before there can be existence. All phenomena in the universe are built upon emptiness; it is the essence which allows for the existence and function of all phenomena. Without emptiness, nothing would come to be through the coming together of conditions, nothing would arise, and nothing would cease.

Emptiness does not mean pessimism and nihilism. Rather, emptiness is creative and constructive. By understanding emptiness we can let go of the attachments that we cling to, and see the world from a different perspective. When we have experienced and directly realized emptiness, we will be in harmony with the entire universe.

Chapter Eight

MIND

The mind is not born and does not die. It is our essence. It is the Dharma body of all Buddhas and the wisdom inherent to all sentient beings. The intrinsic nature of the mind is that which embraces all merit, virtue, and wisdom, and turns away from delusion and attachment. All sentient beings have a mind such as this, but its nature is obscured by ignorance and delusion. When the true mind is known, we will grasp its incredible potential. How can we come to know the mind?

WHERE IS THE MIND?

The mind neither comes nor goes. It has neither direction nor location. It is not inside, nor is it outside. It is not in between. It leaves no trace anywhere. In the *Surangama Sutra*, there is a section in which Ananda, the Buddha's attendant, asks the Buddha about the location of the mind. Ananda proposed seven different locations, and the Buddha refutes each one in turn.

Ananda asks the Buddha, "Does mind reside in the body? Does it reside outside the body? Is it hidden in the eyes? Is the mind located in the darkness of the body? Is it located where causes and conditions come together and where existence arises? Is it located between the six sense organs and the six sense objects? Does it not abide anywhere?" In his answers, the Buddha shows Ananda again and again that mind cannot be located nor pinned to any one of these places. If this is so, then where is the mind located?

The mind does not leave a trace, but when we need it, we see that it is everywhere. There is a Buddhist saying, "The mind is neither inside, outside, nor in between. But the mind is completely present in all states." The mind interpenetrates all things and permeates the ten directions. It is in all places and is present at all times. The mind does not exist in form, nor can any trace of it be found in the material world. That said, there is nowhere that is without the mind, and no time that it does not exist. Where then, do we go to find the mind?

During the Tang dynasty, Chan Master Huairang visited Chan Master Songshan Huian. One day, Huairang asked Huian, "What is the meaning of the patriarch coming from the west?"

Huian turned it around and asked, "Why don't you ask yourself?"

Huairang then asked, "What is the meaning of self?"

Huian replied, "Pure vision of the hidden function."

Huairang inquired, "What is the hidden function?"

Chan Master Huian then opened and closed his eyes. At that moment, Huairang had a great awakening.

What opens and closes are our physical eyes, that which gives the command is the true mind. This mind is not separate from us even for an instant, but its presence is ignored by us most of the time. The mind is called a "hidden function," because its activity is not obvious, and in fact, often exists without our awareness. There is a Buddhist saying that, "If you want to know the 'original self,' see it directly in daily life, for there is no separation."

THE NATURE OF THE MIND

Mind is formless. It has no size, shape, sound, nor smell. It cannot be touched nor held, but when it comes in contact with sense objects it will appear. There is an old Chinese saying, "If you want to understand what the mind is like, it is neither long nor short, neither blue nor white. If you want to see the mind, open your eyes and it is there, close your eyes and it is there. This side is mind and that side is mind."

Mind is our true nature. It is our Buddha nature. The only reason we do not see our own Buddha nature more clearly is because it is obscured by attachment and delusion, like dust that obscures the surface of a mirror. The *Eight Realizations of a Bodhisattva Sutra* says, "The mind is the source of unwholesomeness and the body is a gathering of wrongdoings." When the sutra speaks about the mind in this way, it is referring to the mind that is obscured by defilement and attachment. This is also called the "mind of sentient beings." Alternatively, when the mind faces a situation and does not become attached, but instead remains pure and carefree, this is the true mind, the "Buddha mind."

National Master Zhongfeng (1263-1323) said:

The mind is of several types. The physical mind is part of the body that we inherit from our parents. The conditioned mind creates distinctions between good and bad, and positive and negative in each moment. The spiritual mind is beyond worldly distinctions, is free from confusion, and unchanging. This mind is luminous, preeminent, and unique. The spiritual mind is not greater in sages or lesser among ordinary people. In the ocean of birth and death, it is like a bright pearl that illuminates the sea. On the shore of *nirvana*, it is like a moon that hangs in the sky.

The *Sutra on the Five Kinds of Suffering* says, "The mind leads us to hell, the mind leads us to the realm of hungry ghosts, the mind leads us to the animal realm, and the mind leads us to heaven and the human realm. All actions and appearances are created by the mind. Those who can control their minds are the most powerful. Having struggled with the mind for countless *kalpas*, today I attain Buddhahood and escape from the three realms because of it."

Buddhist sutras use many metaphors and similes to help us understand the nature of the mind. In the following sections, I will discuss ten of these metaphors in some detail:

1. The Mind Is Like a Monkey

The mind is like a monkey, for it is hard to control. There is an old Chinese saying, "the mind is a monkey and thoughts are like horses." Ordinarily the mind is like an energetic and restless monkey. Active by nature, it jumps around and runs wild in the jungle without a moment of rest.

2. The Mind Is Like a Flash of Lightning

The mind is as fast as a flash of lightning or sparks from flint. Nothing moves faster than the mind. From moment to moment, it races through the universe without any obstructions. For example, you may think about traveling to Europe, and in an instant, scenes of Europe will appear in your mind.

3. The Mind Is Like a Wild Deer

The mind is like a wild deer chasing the sense objects. When a deer is thirsty, it goes to a stream. When it is hungry, it searches for grass. The mind is like the wild deer, unable to resist the temptations of the five desires of wealth, sex, fame, food, and sleep, and the six sense objects. It spends most of its time chasing after sights and sounds of the mundane world to fulfill its appetite.

4. The Mind Is Like a Thief

The mind is like a thief, such that it steals our positive karma. The sutras often compare the body to a walled city, the five sense organs to city gates, and our mind to a thief. It carries away our virtue and the merit of our positive karma just as a thief might carry away the hard-earned savings of the people in the town. The Chinese scholar, Wang Yangming (d. 1173) said, "It is easy to capture a bandit in the mountains; it is difficult to catch the thief in the mind." If we can tame the mind, then we will become its master and increase our positive karma.

5. The Mind Is Like an Adversary

The mind is like an adversary, for it causes us suffering. The mind is always causing us trouble. The sutras say, "The nature of negative karma is empty. It is created by the mind. If and when the mind disappears, karma is gone." Some people may feel that their negative karma is very weighty, such that it is permanent or unchangeable. But we know that all phenomena are empty by nature, and the nature of karma is the same. Therefore, we can alter negative karma. If we sincerely repent our wrongdoings, we can lessen the effects of our negative karma. The mind always possesses Buddha nature, pure and at ease. It is only because of delusion that we suffer. If we can eliminate these deluded and destructive thoughts, we can befriend the adversary that is the mind.

6. The Mind Is Like a Servant of Affliction

The mind is like a servant of affliction, for it is ordered about by worldly temptations. The mind is attached to external circumstances, and creates various afflictions. The sutras describe the mind as having three poisons, five hindrances, and eighty-four thousand afflictions. These hindrances and afflictions can cover up our wisdom, restrain the mind, and cause us to lose our clarity and freedom.

7. The Mind Is Like a Powerful King

The mind is like a powerful king, in that it has supreme power over the body. It gives the commands to our eyes, ears, nose, tongue, and body; produces their sensory output; and controls perception.

8. The Mind Is Like an Ever-flowing Spring

The mind is like an ever-flowing spring. It is like China's Yellow River, in that it frequently changes course. Likewise, because of the world's growing energy problems we continue to seek "renewable" energy sources like solar, wind, and hydropower. The mind is like the rushing rivers that power hydroelectric plants; if we can learn how to apply the renewable energy of the mind, we need not fear scarcity.

9. The Mind Is Like a Painter

The *Flower Adornment Sutra* says, "The mind is like an artist. It can paint all things." If the mind is pure and good, it will paint beauty and tranquility. If the mind is defiled and malicious it will paint something monstrous. According to an old Buddhist saying, "Appearances are born from the mind." As the mind becomes a more skillful painter, it can create a world of unlimited beauty and compassion.

10. The Mind Is Like Boundless Space

The nature of the mind is like the vastness of space, in that it can embrace everything. The *Flower Adornment Sutra* says, "If you want to know the state of the Buddha, purify the mind so that it is as vast as space." Space is boundless; it encompasses all without distinction. If we want to understand the state of the Buddhas, we should open our mind so that it extends as far as space, and eliminate any attachments. Then, we will be able to embrace all things and benefit all sentient beings.

Master Dadian (732-824) said, "The mind without delusion is the true mind." When a thought arises in our minds, we should observe it. If the thought arises from purity, equality, compassion, and equanimity, it has arisen from the true mind. If the thought arises from delusion, attachment, jealousy, and arrogance, it has arisen from the defiled mind. Wholesome thoughts come from the true mind; unwholesome thoughts come from the defiled mind. When all of our thoughts are wholesome thoughts, then the true mind is everywhere. But when all of our thoughts are unwholesome thoughts, the true mind will be obscured.

THE WONDROUS BUDDHA MIND

The true mind belongs to everyone. It is also called the "original self," the "Dharma body," and "Buddha nature." No matter what we do, where we go, or what we think, the mind is always in charge, and always with us. When we are hungry, the mind reminds us to eat; when we are thirsty, it reminds us to drink; when the weather turns cold, it reminds us to put on more clothes. The mind cares for us as a mother does. When we see forms or hear sounds, the mind manifests itself, and when we need clothing or food its great strength and kindness carries us.

Chan Master Deshan of Northern China, an expert on the *Diamond Sutra*, wrote the *Blue Dragon Commentary on the Diamond Sutra*. He had heard about the Southern Chan School's method of "sudden enlightenment," and he heartily disagreed with it. Therefore, he decided to go to Southern China and debate this method, carrying the *Blue Dragon Commentary on the Diamond Sutra* with him. On the way, he passed by a small shop. In the shop was a little old lady. Seeing that Deshan wanted to buy some refreshments, she asked him, "What are you carrying on your shoulder?"

Deshan replied, "The Blue Dragon Commentary on the Diamond Sutra."

The old lady said, "Then, let me test you with a question on the Diamond Sutra. If you can answer it, the refreshments will be free."

Deshan confidently agreed.

The old lady continued, "The Diamond Sutra says, 'the mind of the past cannot be obtained, the mind of the present cannot be obtained, and the mind of the future cannot be obtained.' May I ask: which mind wants to eat refreshments?"

Deshan was stunned and did not know how to answer.

How could the true mind be divided into past, present, and future? The thoughts that we have in this very moment are a function of the true mind. The mind is neither obtainable nor nonobtainable. Chan Master Hanshan captures the wondrousness of the mind in a poem:

> My mind is like the autumn moon,
> Clear and bright as a jade pool.
> Nothing compares to its beauty,
> How can I describe it?

Chapter Nine

THE THREE BODIES OF
THE BUDDHA

The Buddha is commonly mentioned in many different contexts. The word "Buddha" can describe the awakened being who lived in India over 2,500 year ago, as well as the Buddha within each one of us. We may begin to wonder, who is the Buddha?

The Buddha was both an ordinary person and an extraordinary person. In one sense he was a sentient being, no different from you or me, who simply did the necessary practice to become a Buddha. In another sense he is a great being who transcends time and space, and pervades all of existence.

One way to understand the Buddha is to learn about the "three bodies," or aspects, of the Buddha. Each of the "three bodies" examines the Buddha from a different perspective. The first body is the Buddha as seen from the perspective of an ordinary person, this is called the "manifested body," or *Nirmanakaya* in Sanskrit. The second body is the Buddha as seen by awakened beings, this is called the "reward body," or *Samboghakaya* in Sanskrit. The third body is the Buddha as part of the universe itself, this is called the "Dharma body," or *Dharmakaya* in Sanskrit. All Buddhas possess these three bodies, for they are three aspects of a unified whole.

The Buddha of our world, Sakyamuni Buddha, appeared as a human being to most people. This was his "manifested body," and through it he taught the Dharma to people on earth. It is called a "manifested body" because it is a physical form that is manifested by the Buddha so that he may appear in the world.

The Buddha's "reward body" is the body which experiences the joy of awakening. Only Buddhas and very advanced bodhisattvas are able to perceive the reward body. The Buddha's "Dharma body" pervades all phenomena of the universe.

THE DHARMA BODY

The Dharma body of the Buddha is one with everything. This is the highest level of truth. Though there are many Buddhas, at this level all Buddhas are the same. The Dharma body is not a "body" in the sense that it is a fixed existence like the reward body or manifested body, for it pervades all of the universe.

The Dharma body is the ultimate truth of all things. It is awakening itself, the supreme reality, the cosmic consciousness that subsumes and includes everything in the universe. The Dharma body is completely pure. It is the union of reason and wisdom. It is omnipresent. To attain awakening and the Dharma body is the ultimate goal of all Buddhist practice. The Dharma body is beyond all duality. The *Flower Adornment Sutra* says, "Dharma nature is fundamentally empty. It cannot be grasped or seen. In its emptiness it is one with the Buddha realm. It cannot be comprehended by mere thought."

Though the true nature of the Dharma body cannot be described in words, it has certain qualities that can be roughly described. Thinking about these qualities can help us reach a deeper understanding of what is meant by the term "Dharma body."

The Dharma body is the unification of reason and principle. It is universal and equally present everywhere. It is the one principle that underlies everything. Within the Dharma body, all distinctions cease.

The Dharma body is the unification of principle and event. All laws and all occurrences of them are unified in the Dharma body. All duality is unified in the Dharma body. The phenomenal universe and its fundamental emptiness are unified in the Dharma body.

The characteristics of the Dharma body are the same as the characteristics of all phenomena. All things in the universe are interconnected. The Dharma body resides in each and every one of them and yet it is not the same as any of them. The Dharma body exists in all times and places without being defined or contained by any of them.

The Dharma body is the same as the intrinsic, pure Buddha nature that resides in all things everywhere. The deluded self can find peace when it understands that it inherently possesses Buddha nature, that this nature pervades all things. Our wish to find what is real and permanent can only be resolved by attaining the Dharma body.

THE REWARD BODY

The Buddha's reward body is the body which enjoys the rewards of awakening. This body clearly shows what are called the "thirty-two marks of excellence" and the "eighty notable characteristics," physical features of the Buddha which are manifestations of his many lifetimes cultivating positive karma, and include such features as golden skin, long slender fingers, and dark blue eyes.

The reward body is both the body that enjoys the delight of awakening and the body that is capable of transmitting the truth of awakening to others. When the Buddhist sutras mention the countless Buddhas that reside in the infinite Buddha realms throughout the universe, they speak of the reward bodies of Buddhas.

Only Buddhas and very advanced bodhisattvas are capable of seeing a Buddha's reward body. Amitabha Buddha or the Medicine Buddha are examples of reward bodies that are frequently portrayed in Buddhist art. Sakyamuni Buddha has a reward body that exists in this world, but very few people are pure enough to see it.

THE MANIFESTED BODY

A Buddha's manifested body is the body he uses to teach the Dharma within the world. This body is a compassionate projection of his reward body. When Sakymuni Buddha arose in this world, he was already an awakened Buddha. He arose as a manifested body for the purpose of leading sentient beings toward the truth. Buddhas do not appear within the six realms of existence in the full splendor of their reward bodies because, if they did, no one would feel they are able to accomplish the practice necessary to attain awakening for the Buddha's achievements would seem so far beyond what ordinary people are capable of.

The manifested body of the Buddha is a skillful means to show us that it is essential to persevere towards awakening. Sakyamuni Buddha used his manifested body to reside in Tusita Heaven, enter his mother's womb, be born in the world, renounce the home life, defeat Mara, attain awakening, teach the Dharma, and enter final *nirvana*, each to lead us closer to the truth.

Many people wish that they could see and learn from the Buddha right now, and wonder why the manifested body of the Buddha cannot have the incredible longevity of the reward body. There are several reasons for this. First, the manifested body appears on earth for the sole purpose of leading sentient beings toward awakening. It appears only when conditions are right. As soon as the Buddha has brought those who are ready to awakening and planted the proper seeds in those who are not yet ready, then the conditions which brought him to the world have dissipated and he departs.

Second, the Buddha does not remain to show us the truth that all things are impermanent. His manifested body comes to an end so that we may learn to look beyond our reverence for it to the even greater perfection of the Dharma body.

Third, by not remaining on earth, the Buddha emphasizes that awakening depends on our own effort, not on his. When we understand this we will be inspired to redouble our efforts to learn the Dharma.

Fourth, the Buddha does not remain on earth so that we gain a sense of how precious and valuable his teachings are and how easy it is to miss the chance to hear them. This should show us just how compassionate the Buddha is, and how the Dharma is taught solely to liberate sentient beings from suffering.

HOW THE THREE BODIES ARE INTERRELATED

A Buddha's manifested body and his reward body are both dependent on the Dharma body, which underlies everything in the

universe. To say this, however, does not mean that we should al-
low ourselves to oversimplify and blur these three aspects of the
Buddha into one. The distinctions between the three bodies of the
Buddha point us towards distinctions within our own minds.

There are three basic distinctions between a Buddha's reward
body and the Dharma body. First, the reward body has form and
can be perceived by highly advanced bodhisattvas. In contrast, the
Dharma body has no particular form, for it both includes and transcends all things everywhere.

Second, though a Buddha's reward body can be perceived by
some bodhisattvas, it is not perceived in the same way by each
of them. In contrast, the Dharma body is immutable: it is beyond
change, beyond transformation, and beyond all signs and appearance. One cannot have an individual perception of the Dharma
body, because the Dharma body transcends all individuality.

Third, a Buddha's reward body is so special it creates a field
around it. This field is the Pure Land of that Buddha. Pure Lands
can be perceived and experienced by the many different kinds of
sentient beings that are drawn to them. In contrast, the Pure Land
of the Dharma body is something that only a Buddha can know.

Just as there are three basic distinctions between a Buddha's
reward body and the Dharma body, so there are three important
distinctions between a Buddha's reward body and his manifested
body. A Buddha's reward body creates its own Pure Land around it
and draws sentient beings toward it. In contrast, a Buddha's manifested body appears in a world according to the collective karma of
the sentient beings living there. The *Lotus Sutra* says that a Buddha
"teaches the Dharma and manifests in the form that will be most
effective for liberating" the people who will see it. The body referred to in this quotation is the Buddha's manifested body.

Wherever that body appears, it will be seen according to the customs and expectations of the beings in that realm. If a Buddha appears in heaven, he will be seen as a heavenly being. If he appears in the human realm, he will be seen to have a human body. If he appears in the animal realm, he will be seen as an animal. And if he appears in the hell realm, he will be seen to have a body suitable to that realm.

Second, a Buddha's manifested body cannot experience the fullness of awakening in the same way that his reward body can. A Buddha's manifested body is a particular fulfillment of the karma of the beings in a certain realm. For this reason, it is also limited by the conditions of the realm in which it appears. For example, Sakyamuni Buddha had to endure headaches, back pain, insults, bad food, physical assaults, and death.

Third, a Buddha's manifested body is limited by the comprehension of the beings of the realm in which it appears. For example, the manifested body of Sakyamuni Buddha as he appeared to people in our world did not have all of the sublime features of his reward body.

When we take refuge in the Triple Gem, at the most profound level we are taking refuge in nothing more than our own intrinsic nature. The truth lies within us already. The Dharma is a teaching designed to help us discover our intrinsic nature. The manifested body of Sakyamuni Buddha provides us with an example of how to live and how to achieve liberation from suffering in this world. As we follow that example, we will learn how to draw on the strength and wisdom of the Dharma body.

The Dharma body lies within us like the clear blue sky, or like the sun or the moon. In and of itself, it is always pure and undefiled. We lose sight of it only when the clouds of our own greed, anger, and ignorance obscure our view. We can discover the pure Dharma body that dwells within us by always turning our attention to our own best impulses. Whenever we are virtuous and compassionate, we interact with the Dharma body. Whenever we are inspired by the example of Sakyamuni Buddha, we are inspired by the Dharma body.

The great Chan Master Linji summed up our relationship to the three bodies of the Buddha in this way: "We enter upon the Dharma body of the Buddha the moment our minds are filled with the light of perfect purity. We enter upon the reward body of the Buddha the moment our minds are filled with the light that transcends all distinctions. We enter upon the manifested body of the Buddha the moment our minds are filled with the light of pure discernment."

Chapter Ten

BUDDHA NATURE

Each of us has been endowed with Buddha nature from the very beginning, though we may not know it. It is one of the saddest things about us that so many do not know themselves, nor can they recognize their original face. Every day, we are able to call out our friends' names, but we do not know who we are.

We study Buddhism in order to know ourselves, to respect ourselves, and to affirm ourselves. The Buddhist sutras say that all beings have Buddha nature within, and that it cannot be sought outside of ourselves. When the Buddha attained awakening under the bodhi tree, he said, "Marvelous, marvelous! All sentient beings have the Tathagata's wisdom and virtue, but they fail to realize it because they cling to deluded thoughts and attachments."

Once the Buddha held an assembly on Vulture Peak, and held out a brilliant, wish-fulfilling *mani* pearl, and presented it to the four heavenly kings, saying, "Look at this *mani* pearl and tell me, what color is it?"

The four heavenly kings each answered differently: one said blue, one said yellow, one said red, and one said white.

The Buddha took back the *mani* pearl. Then he opened his hand again and asked, "What color is the *mani* pearl?"

The four heavenly kings did not understand. One said, "Lord Buddha, there is no *mani* pearl in your hand."

The Buddha said, "When I showed you an ordinary pearl, you could all distinguish its color. But when the true *mani* pearl is before you, you do not see it."

The wisdom and merit of the Buddha and the true *mani* pearl are both like our own Buddha nature—we live with it every day but do not recognize it even when it is right in front of our eyes.

UNCHANGING NATURE

The Sanskrit word *prakrti*, "nature," refers to what is unchanging. Nature, form, and cultivation are all related, but while form and cultivation are subject to change, nature is unchanging. *Prakrti* refers to something's "intrinsic nature," the original quality or essence of phenomena. Regarding phenomena with form, it refers to the innate quality of sentient beings. Intrinsic nature is that quality that cannot be changed by external forces and is present throughout the universe. It is the root of all phenomena. It is also known as Buddha nature, the Dharma body, the pure body of intrinsic nature, Tathagata nature, the nature of awakening, and the inherent nature of the Buddha.

All phenomena in the universe lack an independent self, and as such are constantly changing. Just as the universe goes through formation, abiding, decline, and destruction; people have birth, aging, sickness, and death; and the mind has arising, abiding, changing, and ceasing. Only the original nature of phenomena and our own original face do not change.

Sentient beings travel throughout the ten dharma realms within the cycle of birth and death, transmigrating endlessly from the hell realm, hungry ghost realm, animal realm, human realm, *asura* realm, and heavenly realm, as well as the four noble realms of *sravakas*, *pratyekabuddhas*, bodhisattvas, and Buddhas. Each being's form of existence continues to change, but the nature of the mind does not change. It is similar to how a single piece of gold can be made into rings, bracelets, or earrings: even though it may take on many different forms, the nature of the gold has not been altered. Even as sentient beings travel in the cycle of birth and death, their Buddha nature remains the same.

When the Sixth Chan Patriarch, Huineng (638-713), was near death, all of his disciples who heard this news wept. Only Master Shenhui (668-760) remained calm and composed. So Master Huineng said:

> Only the young monk Shenhui understands wholesome and unwholesome. Unmoved by slander and fame, he is neither sad nor happy. The rest of you have yet to understand this. You have spent all these years here, what Way have you cultivated? For whom are you shedding your tears? If you are concerned that I do not know where I am going, I assure you that I know where I am going. If I did not know where I was going, I would not have notified you. You cry because you do not know where I am going. If you knew, you would not cry. Dharma nature is inherently without birth and death, or coming and going.

That is why Manorhita, the Twenty-second Indian Patriarch, said:

> The mind turns, following all things;
> Though this turning can be tranquil.
> Recognize the nature of this flow
> And be without joy and without sorrow.

DIFFERENT NAMES FOR BUDDHA NATURE

The Buddhist sutras use many different names for Buddha nature. Master Jizang (549-623), in his *Treatise on the Profound Mahayana*, said, "The sutras speak of 'bright nature,' 'Dharma nature,' 'suchness,' 'reality,' and so on. All of these are different terms for Buddha nature." He also said, "Buddha nature has many names including 'Dharma nature,' '*nirvana*,' '*prajna*,' 'one vehicle,' '*surangama samadhi*,' and 'lion's roar *samadhi*.' It is said that the great sage follows conditions and applies skillful means. That is why there are so many names throughout the various sutras."

The following is a short list of names for Buddha nature in the sutras:

- The *Bodhisattva Precepts Sutra* calls Buddha nature the "mind ground," for this "ground" can give rise to infinite goodness.

- The *Mahaprajnaparamita Sutra* calls Buddha nature "bodhi," which means "awakened." It is because the essence of Buddha nature is awakening.

- The *Flower Adornment Sutra* calls Buddha nature the "Dharma realm," because Buddha nature unifies and embraces everything in the universe.

- The *Diamond Sutra* calls Buddha nature *"Tathagata,"* which is usually translated as "thus come," because Buddha nature comes from nowhere.

- The *Mahaprajnaparamita Sutra* also calls Buddha nature *"nirvana,"* for *nirvana* is where all sages will return.

- The *Golden Light Sutra* calls Buddha nature *"Tathagata"* because Buddha nature is truly eternal and unchanging.

- The *Vimalakirti Sutra* calls Buddha nature the Dharma body, because it is what the other bodies of the Buddha, the reward body and the manifested body, rely upon.

- The *Treatise on Awakening of Faith in Mahayana* calls Buddha nature the "true essence," because Buddha nature does not arise and is not extinguished.

- The *Mahaparinirvana Sutra* calls Buddha nature "the Buddha essence," because Buddha nature is the essence of the three bodies of the Buddha.

- The *Complete Enlightenment Sutra* calls Buddha nature the "universal embracing and upholding," because all merits and virtues flow from Buddha nature.

- The *Lion's Roar of Queen Srimala Sutra* calls Buddha nature the "storehouse of the Tathagata," because Buddha nature conceals, covers, and embraces all things.

- The *Sutra of Supreme Meaning* calls Buddha nature "perfect awakening," because Buddha nature can break through the darkness and illuminate all things.

Buddha nature is another case of "one teaching with a thousand names" so that it can respond to all circumstances.

The Chinese philosopher Mencius said, "The mouth turns to taste, the eye to form, the ear to sound, the nose to smell, the four limbs to peace and quiet. These are their natures." When the eyes see, the ears hear, the nose smells, the tongue tastes, the body acts, or the mind knows, these are all functions of the true mind. Whether we are sitting or sleeping, speaking or staying silent, moving or standing still, carrying water or hauling firewood, receiving guests or sending someone off, all come from Buddha nature.

The *Treasure Record of the Chan School* says, "In the womb, it was the body. In the world, it was a human being. In the eyes, it sees. In the ears, it hears. In the nose, it smells. In the mouth, it speaks. In the hands, it grasps. In the feet, it moves. It appears throughout the dharma realms; it is contained in a speck of dust. Those who know call it Buddha nature. Those who do not know call it 'spirit' or 'soul.'"

THE EQUALITY OF BUDDHA NATURE

The Buddha said, "All sentient beings will eventually attain complete awakening. That is why I have said, 'All sentient beings have Buddha nature.'"

Master Huineng went from Xinhui in Guangdong Province to Huangmei in Hubei Province to ask Master Hongren to become his teacher. When Master Huineng first met Master Hongren, the first thing Hongren asked him was, "Where are you from? What do you seek?"

"I am a commoner from Xinzhou in Lingnan. I have traveled far to pay homage to you. I seek to be a Buddha and nothing else."

The Fifth Patriarch asked, "You are from Lingnan and also a barbarian! How do you expect to be a Buddha?"

Huineng then said, "Though people may be northerners or southerners, Buddha nature has no north or south. While this barbarian's body is different from yours, Venerable Master, what difference is there in Buddha nature?"

Although people are called northerners and southerners, wealthy and poor, Buddha nature does not have a south, north, wealthy, or poor. For all people, Buddha nature is equal. Buddha nature is found in all sentient beings just as both the tall trees and short plants are enriched by rainfall. All sentient beings have Buddha nature, and Buddha nature is equal in all.

The *Mahayana Stopping and Seeing Method* states:

If the essence of the mind is equal in all, there is no cultivation and no non-cultivation, achievement and non-achievement, or awakening and non-awakening. In order to understand the Buddha as he is, the word "awakening" is used. Again, if the essence of the mind is equal, there is no difference among sentient beings, Buddhas, and mind. Therefore, the verses in the sutra say, "The mind, the Buddha, and sentient beings are not different." Since the mind creates dharma realms due to dependent

origination and Dharma nature is not destroyed, this results in the truths of eternal equality and eternal differentiation. Because of eternal equality, mind, Buddhas, and
sentient beings are the same. Because of eternal differentiation, when churning in the five realms of existence, our
nature is called "sentient being." When returning to the
origin, it is called "Buddha."

Master Daoxin (580-651), the Fourth Patriarch of the Chan
School, lived on Mount Shuangfeng. On the mountain dwelled an
old woodcutter who wished to become a monk under the Chan
master. Master Daoxin told him, "You are already too old. If you
want to become a monk, you can wait until your next life."

The old man then left the master and walked to a stream where
he saw a young woman washing clothes. The old man asked her,
"Miss, may I stay the night?"

The young woman answered, "I have to ask my parents."

"I just need your permission, and it'll be all right," the old man
said.

Just like that, the young virgin became pregnant. Because her
parents felt that she had ruined their reputation, they kicked her out
of the house. The young woman survived by begging. Eventually,
she gave birth to a son.

Some years later on Huangmei road, Master Daoxin encountered the little boy. This child requested to become a monk.

The Chan master said, "You are too young. How can you become a monk?"

"Master," the child said, "in the past, you said I was too old.
Now you accuse me of being too young. When are you willing to
let me become a monk under you?"

The Chan master suddenly had a realization. He immediately asked, "What is your name? Where do you live?"

"I am called 'the boy with no name.' My home is on Shili Alley."

"Everyone has a name," the master said. "why do you not?"

The boy answered, "I take 'Buddha nature' as my name, so I do not have a name." This boy without a name would later be known as Master Hongren, the Fifth Patriarch of the Chan School.

In Buddhism, the doctrine of "eternal differentiation" refers to karma operating in the past, present, and future, and rebirth among the five realms of existence. It is because of differences like this that the Chan master could say, "If you are too old, I don't want you. If you are too young, it is not right." However, when the "boy with no name" took Buddha nature as his name, he demonstrated that he understood the eternal and unchanging characteristics of nature. This is "eternal equality."

In the *Record of Wanling*, Master Huangbo (d. 850) says, "The patriarch directly pointed out that the original mind of all sentient beings is the nature of the Buddhas, which does not need to be cultivated, does not have any levels, and is neither dark nor bright. The mind is the Buddha. From the Buddhas down to beings with less sentience, all possess Buddha nature and have the same essence of mind. Therefore, Bodhidharma came from the West and transmitted only one Dharma. He pointed out that all sentient beings are essentially Buddhas and do not need to cultivate. Today, aside from recognizing the mind and seeing one's intrinsic nature, you must not seek from others."

In the *Lotus Sutra*, whenever Sadaparibhuta Bodhisattva was bullied, hurt, insulted, or scolded by others, he not only did not get mad, but he would respectfully say, "I dare not disrespect you, for

I regard you all as Buddhas." From his example, we should understand that the equality of Buddha nature means that respecting others is the same as respecting oneself.

AWAKENING AND BUDDHA NATURE

The *Treatise on Awakening of Faith in the Mahayana* says, "The one Dharma is the one mind. This one mind embraces all mundane and supramundane teachings. It is the teaching of the one dharma realm embracing all phenomena. It is only because of delusions that there are distinctions. Away from delusion, all that is left are things as they are [suchness]." This means that as long as all sentient beings can stay away from and eliminate all delusions, they are Buddhas with pure intrinsic nature.

There was once a student monk who went to the home of National Master Nanyang Huizhong (d. 775) to study with him. He asked for instruction, saying, "The mind is not greater in the Buddhas and not less in ordinary people. The patriarchs changed the term 'mind' to 'nature.' Please Chan master, what is the difference between 'mind' and 'nature'?"

National Master Huizhong said, "When we are ignorant, there are distinctions. When we awaken, there are no distinctions."

The student monk then asked, "Buddha nature is permanent. The mind is impermanent. Why do you say that there is no difference?"

Huizhong said, "You are depending only on the words and not depending on the meaning. Consider water: when it is cold, water becomes ice. When it is warm, ice becomes water. When you are ignorant, your nature freezes into mind. When you awaken, your mind melts into nature. Mind and nature are one and the same. It is only due to ignorance and awakening that there is a difference."

In the *Diamond Sutra*, the Buddha says, *"Prajnaparamita* is not *prajnaparamita* and that is what is called *prajnaparamita."* This means that what is Dharma is not Dharma, and what is not Dharma is Dharma. This may sound like a contradiction, but whether something is the Dharma or not depends upon whether one is ignorant or awakened.

One day, Chan Master Danxia Tianran of the Tang dynasty stayed overnight at a Buddhist temple. It was winter, and it was very cold. Danxia took a wooden statue of the Buddha and threw it into the fire. When the discipline master saw this, he shouted, "You should die for that! How dare you take the Buddha statue and burn it to stay warm?"

Danxia said, "I am not burning it to stay warm. I am burning it to obtain relics."

The discipline master said, "Nonsense! How could a wooden statue have relics?"

"Since it is wood and has no relics, why don't you bring me more to burn?"

Chan Master Danxia already understood dependent origination and the emptiness of nature, so in his mind the Dharma body of the Buddha pervades the universe. The discipline master only recognized the Buddha as a wooden statue. Due to his one thought of ignorance, what was once the pure Dharma becomes impure mundane Dharma. Therefore, we say that Dharma is not Dharma.

Another Chan story illustrates this point. One day, Chan Master Panshan Baoji (720-814) of Youzhou Province was walking past a marketplace. Suddenly, he heard an exchange that caused him to awaken.

A patron said to a butcher, "Sir, cut me a piece of good meat!" The butcher laid down his knife. Hands on his hips, he said, "Dear fellow, tell me, which piece is not good?"

All phenomena arise from dependent origination. They are all equal, without distinction or duality. With a single awakened thought, impure Dharma with outflows can become pure, supramundane Dharma without outflows. While the ignorant mind is mastered by the world, the awakened mind turns the world. The difference between ignorance and awakening can lie in a single transcendent thought. This is a matter of cultivating the mind, not oral debate. From something as mundane as selling meat, the Chan master was able to realize the truth that all phenomena's nature is equal and without duality. In this way, what is not Dharma is Dharma.

While a young person was meditating, an old Chan master happened to walk by. The young man did not rise to greet him, so the Chan master said, "You saw me coming, and yet you ignored me? Such impoliteness."

The young monk, imitating the Chan master's tone of voice, said, "Sitting to greet you is the same as standing to greet you."

When the old Chan master heard this, he immediately stepped forward and slapped the young man on each side of the face. After the young man was smacked, he held his face in his hands and protested, "Why did you hit me?"

The old Chan master, as if nothing had happened, said, "When I hit you, it is not hitting you."

Another story illustrates how much emphasis Chan masters place on understanding Buddha nature. When Master Heze Shenhui first met the Sixth Patriarch Huineng, Huineng asked, "This Dharma friend has endured much to make the long journey here. Did what is inherent come as well? If you have what is inherent, you should know its master. Try to speak of it."

Shenhui said, "I take non-abiding as what is inherent, as seeing is its master."

The patriarch said, "What this novice said is so careless!"

Shenhui asked in return, "Master, when you sit in meditation, do you see it or not?"

The patriarch hit Shenhui three times with his staff and asked, "When I hit you, do you feel the pain or not?"

Shenhui said, "I both feel the pain and do not feel the pain."

The patriarch said, "I both see and do not see."

Shenhui asked, "What does it mean to both see and not see?"

The patriarch replied, "This is what I see: I constantly see my mind's wrongdoing. I do not see others' right and wrong or wholesome and unwholesome. This is seeing and not seeing. What do you mean when you claim both pain and no pain? If you do not feel pain, then you are the same as a piece of wood or stone. If you feel pain, then you are no different from an ordinary person who responds to it with anger. Your earlier reference to seeing and not seeing is dualistic; feeling or not feeling pain is arising and ceasing. Your intrinsic nature is yet to be seen, yet you play tricks on others."

When a person who has yet to awaken imitates the speech of an awakened being, it is much like the above. Shenhui's question of "seeing or not seeing" is simply two kinds of attachment. Pain and non-pain are simply arising and ceasing. Buddha nature is what transcends all. To sever the two sides, to not distinguish between the good and the bad, is to truly see nature. This is the difference between ignorance and awakening.

Why are sentient beings ignorant? Because their Buddha nature has been obscured by delusion. Buddha nature is like the openness of a clear, blue sky. It is like a perfectly clear mirror that has been covered by the dust of affliction and ignorance, and as such can no longer reflect a perfect image. When this occurs for each of us, we fall into the ocean of birth and death, and suffer.

SEE ONE'S NATURE, BECOME A BUDDHA

The *Platform Sutra* says, "What is meant by 'non-thought?' It means to know all phenomena without attachment. Non-thought is using the mind to reach everywhere without being attached anywhere. Purify the inherent mind and allow the six consciousnesses to exit through the six sense organs onto the six sense objects without attachment or integration. Come and go freely, and circulate without obstruction; this is *prajna samadhi,* liberating and carefree, and is the practice of non-thought."

These passages describe "non-thought," an aim of Chan practitioners. When faced with anything they should not cling to it nor reject it. They should follow conditions naturally, so that they can enjoy freedom and liberation. This is what it means to "see one's nature and become a Buddha."

Chan Master Huangbo Xiyun said, "If practitioners want to attain Buddhahood, they do not need to learn all teachings. They only need to learn not to seek and not to attach. Without seeking, the mind does not arise. Without attaching, the mind does not cease. Non-arising and non-ceasing is the Buddha. We must understand that all phenomena are created in the mind. Today, learn no-mind, eliminate all conditions, do not give rise to delusions and distinctions, eliminate the distinction between self and others, be without greed or anger, be without hatred or love, be without winning or losing, and eliminate as many delusions as possible.

Intrinsic nature is pure. This is the Way of cultivating *bodhi*. If you do not understand this and do not know the original mind, even if you widely study, diligently cultivate, and even if you eat rough food and wear coarse clothing, you are on the wrong path."

When you can attain the state without seeking and attachments, and the state in which all delusions are eliminated, you will see your own nature and become a Buddha.

Chapter Eleven

NIRVANA

The profound teachings of Buddhism are often misunderstood, and this has been the case for thousands of years. For example, *nirvana*, the goal of all Buddhist practitioners, is mistaken by many people to simply be the same as death. Actually, *nirvana* is not death. It is a transcendent state that is completely different from death.

In most Buddhist temples, statues of the Buddha are generally portrayed in one of three positions: either standing, sitting, or lying down. His sitting position symbolizes meditative concentration and peace. His standing position symbolizes his active nature, by which he taught the Dharma. His reclining position symbolizes *nirvana*. This position embodies the unity of the Buddha's peaceful and active natures. In *nirvana*, the Buddha has transcended time and space, all duality, all relative points of view, all delusion, all birth and death. In *nirvana* he is one with the Dharma realm, the great body of the universe. *Nirvana* is not death, nor is it the obliteration of consciousness. *Nirvana* is truth, the highest level of realization, and the ultimate goal of Buddhist practice.

THE MEANING OF NIRVANA

In Sanskrit, the word *nirvana* means "cessation," "liberation," "tranquility," and "non-arising." The *Mahaparinirvana Sutra* says, "The end of all defilement is *nirvana*." The *Treatise on the Great Compendium of the Abhidharma* says that *nirvana* is, "The elimination of all afflictions, the extinguishing of the three fires [of greed, anger, and ignorance], the extinction of the three aspects of [arising, abiding, and ceasing], and the leaving of all realms of existence." The *Samyukta Agama* says *nirvana* is "The eternal end of greed, the eternal end of anger, the eternal end of ignorance, and the eternal end of all afflictions." *Nirvana* is the third of the Four Noble Truths: a world in which greed, anger, ignorance, wrong views, duality, and affliction are all extinguished. *Nirvana* is tranquility, purity, and the transcendence of the distinction between oneself and others.

When the Buddha attained awakening under the bodhi tree, he awakened to the truth of the universe and attained *nirvana*. *Nirvana* is our pure, intrinsic nature. It is the true "self." *Nirvana* allows us to eliminate the tension between the self and others, and transcend the obstructions of space and time. We will not be bound by afflictions, suffering, duality, differentiation, and hardships, and we will not be trapped in the cycle of birth and death. If we can enter this awakened state, we will transcend birth and death into liberation.

DIFFERENT NAMES FOR NIRVANA

Nirvana is described in many ways throughout the Buddhist sutras and commentaries, and one of the most common ways is through describing what *nirvana* is not. The *Treatise on Abhidharma-skandha-pada* describes *nirvana* by saying it is "non-action, non-abiding, non-doing, without boundaries, without outflow, without arising, without expiring, without beginning, without defilements..." The *Treatise on the Four Noble Truths* describes *nirvana* by saying that it is "without destroying, without loss, without equal, without hindrance, without desire, without anything above it, without limit, without attachment..."

In terms of positive descriptions, the *Treatise on Abhidharma-skandha-pada* describes *nirvana* as "truth, the other shore, marvelous, tranquil, eternal, secure, supreme, the most wholesome, and unique." The *Treatise on the Four Noble Truths* describes *nirvana* positively as "liberation, transcendent, the one and only, complete, pure, supreme, truth, suchness..." These are affirming descriptions that give *nirvana* broader interpretations.

In addition to these descriptions, the *Mahaparinirvana Sutra* says that *nirvana* is Buddha nature. The *Flower Adornment Sutra* says that *nirvana* is the intrinsic nature of all phenomena. The *Mahaprajnaparamita Sutra* says that *nirvana* is "*Prajna* that is beyond common knowledge and knows everything." The *Surangama Sutra* says that *nirvana* is "the truth in which activity and stillness cease." The *Vimalakirti Sutra* says that *nirvana* is the "the ten grounds of Dharma method of non-duality." The *Lion's Roar of Queen Srimala Sutra* tells us that *nirvana* is the "storehouse of the Tathagata" and "the inherently pure mind." *Nirvana* is intrinsic nature that does not arise or cease.

Kumarajiva, the great translator of Chinese Buddhist texts, translated *nirvana* into Chinese as *miedu* (滅度). *Mie* means to extinguish the hindrance of defilements, and *du* means to cross the ocean of birth and death to the other shore. Xuanzang, another great translator, translated *nirvana* as *yuanji* (圓寂). *Yuan* means complete and perfect, and *ji* means tranquility. Though *nirvana* has been translated in many different ways, it simply means to possess all virtues and eliminate one's afflictions and habitual tendencies.

SPECIAL CHARACTERISTICS OF NIRVANA

Though there have been many different explanations and interpretations of *nirvana* over time, the truth of *nirvana* never changes. *Nirvana* is always our pure, intrinsic nature and the essence of reality. This nature and essence is not greater in sages, nor is less in ordinary people.

The *Universal Parinirvana Sutra* says that *nirvana* has eight characteristics:

1. *Ever present. Nirvana* permeates the past, present, and future and always exists. It pervades in all directions and always abides in the universe.

2. *Cessation and tranquility.* In the state of *nirvana*, birth and death are extinguished. It is a state of total tranquility.

3. *Eternity.* Because it does not move, change, increase, or decrease, it is said to be eternal.

4. *Deathless.* Since *nirvana* never arises and never ceases, it is without death.

5. *Purity. Nirvana* is a state in which all hindrances have been purified.

6. *Ubiquity.* Because it permeates everything without difficulty, *nirvana* is omnipresent.

7. *Non-action. Nirvana* is the most wondrous state beyond all action. Therefore, it is called "non-action."

8. *Joy.* There is no more suffering from birth and death in the state of *nirvana*, and only eternal happiness remains.

In the Buddhist sutras, similes and metaphors are also used to describe the state of *nirvana*. Ten of these comparisons are:

1. *Nirvana is like a lotus flower.* A lotus flower cannot grow away from mud, but it is also not soiled by the mud. *Nirvana* is like the lotus flower. It is not defiled by any afflictions, but it cannot be attained apart from the cycle of birth and death.

2. *Nirvana is like water. Nirvana* has the refreshing and cleansing qualities of water; it can extinguish the fire and suffering of afflictions. Just as water can quench thirst, *nirvana* can end all desires.

3. *Nirvana is like an antidote for all poisons. Nirvana* is like the medicine that can cure all afflictions. Therefore, *nirvana* is the refuge for all sentient beings who are suffering from the poisons of defilements and afflictions.

4. *Nirvana is like the great ocean.* The great ocean can embrace all things without differentiation. *Nirvana* too has

no attachment to love or hatred, and as such is far away from defilement. The ocean is vast and does not differentiate between this shore and that shore, and it can embrace a thousand rivers without ever becoming full. Likewise, *nirvana* is also vast and without boundaries. It can embrace all sentient beings without ever becoming full.

5. *Nirvana is like food.* Food can satisfy our hunger and sustain us. Similarly, *nirvana* can wipe out the hunger and weaknesses of our suffering, and calm the worries and anxieties of sentient beings.

6. *Nirvana is like space. Nirvana* is a state that is without birth and death, without coming and going, and without attachments. Likewise, space is without boundaries and limits. It abides nowhere and pervades everywhere. It does not depend on anything, but everything relies on it.

7. *Nirvana is like a mani pearl.* It can radiate a virtuous glow and bring joy to all sentient beings.

8. *Nirvana is like sandalwood.* Sandalwood is a kind of precious wood. *Nirvana* is like sandalwood in that it can give off the fragrance of the precepts, with which nothing can compare. *Nirvana* exceeds all other things in the world.

9. *Nirvana is like the wind.* A gust of wind can carry a sailboat across the sea. Likewise, the wonderful quality of *nirvana* can blow people towards awakening.

10. *Nirvana is like a mountain peak.* It stands firm amidst the wind and storms, and stands so tall that the thieves of defilement cannot climb up to the top. On the peak, the seeds of suffering and ignorance cannot grow.

THE DIFFERENT KINDS OF NIRVANA

There are different kinds of *nirvana*, and the different schools of Buddhism categorize *nirvana* in more than one way. The following section examines the classifications of *nirvana* from the Tiantai and the Consciousness-Only schools.

Threefold Nirvana of the Tiantai School

The Tiantai School classifies and interprets *nirvana* from three aspects: its essence, appearance, and function.

1. *Pure nirvana of inherent nature.* The essence of *nirvana* is the same as all phenomena: it is pure, and does not arise or cease.

2. *Perfectly pure nirvana.* In appearance *nirvana* is perfectly pure, for it is the fruit of cultivation in which the nature of all phenomena is truly realized and all defilements are completely purified.

3. *Skillfully pure nirvana.* In terms of function, *nirvana* is the skillful means by which the Buddha teaches all sentient beings. To liberate sentient beings, the Buddha's manifested body taught the Dharma in accordance with the different conditions of sentient beings. When the right conditions

ceased, his manifested body entered *nirvana*. But, in reality birth is not truly birth and death is not truly death. Birth and death are simply aspects of the skillful means of *nirvana*.

Fourfold Nirvana of the Consciousness-Only School

The Consciousness-Only School categorizes *nirvana* into four kinds:

1. *Pure nirvana of inherent nature.* Though all phenomena are shrouded by defilment, the nature of phenomena is always pure and unchanging, and does not arise or cease. Intrinsic nature has immeasurable merit and virtue, and is equally possessed by all sentient beings. Intrinsic nature is different from all phenomena, and is also not different from all phenomena. Sentient beings need not seek pure intrinsic nature from outside.

2. *Nirvana with remainder.* Those who have attained *nirvana* with remainder have cut off the defilements of the three realms and create no new karma. However, their physical body that resulted from past karma still exists, though it is no longer influenced by hunger, cold, suffering, or joy. Those who have attained *nirvana* with remainder always maintain a state of tranquility.

3. *Nirvana without remainder.* Those who have attained *nirvana* without remainder have not only cut off all defilements, but the physical body no longer exists. All remnants of past karma are gone.

4. *Non-abiding nirvana.* Those who have attained non-abid-
    ing *nirvana* have cut off the hindrance of attachment to
    knowledge, and have realized the truth that there is no dif-
    ference between the cycle of birth and death and *nirvana.*
    Therefore they have no aversion to the cycle of birth and
    death. They return to suchness, and have no attachment to
    abiding in *nirvana.* They use their great compassion and
    wisdom to benefit all sentient beings.

From the classifications described above, we can see that one
does not need to wait until death to achieve the state of *nirvana.*
The life of the Buddha provides a good example of this. When the
Buddha was thirty-one years of age, he achieved *nirvana* while sitting under the bodhi tree. However, his physical body that was the
result of past karma still existed. This came to be known as *"nirvana* with remainder." When he was eighty years old, he passed
away under twin sala trees, achieving *nirvana* without remainder.
During the forty-nine years of traveling to various places to teach
the Dharma and liberate sentient beings, he lived a life without
delusion and without attachment. This is non-abiding *nirvana.*

In the *Lotus Sutra*, the Buddha says about himself, "I became
a Buddha many *kalpas* ago. From that time on, I have stayed in
this world to teach the Dharma and liberate others. I also traveled to countless other worlds to guide and benefit sentient beings." That the Buddha was born, renounced, defeated the Mara,
attained Buddhahood, taught the Dharma, and entered *nirvana*
is a function of "skillfully pure *nirvana."* This is also the state of
non-abiding *nirvana.* So, if we are seeking to attain *nirvana,* we
must find our intrinsic nature. This is the "pure *nirvana* of inherent nature."

THE STATE OF NIRVANA

Every day, sentient beings suffer from their own ignorance and desire for wealth, sex, fame, food and drink, and sleep, as well as the six sense objects of sights, sounds, smells, tastes, touch, and *dharmas*. But in what state do Buddhas and bodhisattvas who have attained *nirvana* dwell? According to the *Nirvana Sutra of the Northern Tradition*, *nirvana* has four qualities:

1. *Permanent.* Nirvana is an awakened state that never changes. It is permanent.

2. *Blissful.* Nirvana is said to have four kinds of bliss: the bliss of no suffering, the bliss of great tranquility, the bliss of great wisdom, and the bliss that cannot be destroyed. In the ordinary world, happiness is conditional, as it is tempered by suffering. The state of *nirvana* transcends both suffering and happiness. It is the absolute, perfect bliss of being free from suffering. *Nirvana* is also beyond language, words, and thought. There is bliss with great tranquility because *nirvana* transcends the confusion and chaos of different points of view. After the Buddhas and Tathagatas attain *nirvana*, they gain great wisdom. Free from delusion, they can truly understand the truth of all teachings. After the Tathagatas attain *nirvana*, their Dharma body becomes as indestructible as a diamond, and cannot be destroyed.

3. *Pure.* In *nirvana*, delusions and defilements are extinguished. This state is perfectly clear and pure.

4. *True Self.* When one attains the state of *nirvana*, the self is completely free, without limits or attachments. This kind of self is the true self.

Nirvana is without arising, without abiding, without a temporary self, and lacks nothing. It is the ultimate state that ends the accumulation of all suffering. It is the world that eliminates craving, abandons clinging, and ends desires and afflictions. To enter *nirvana* is to enter the blissful land of complete virtue.

HOW TO ATTAIN NIRVANA

Nirvana transcends all duality. It cannot be attained through worldly experience, knowledge, or learning. It can only be attained through one's own cultivation and realization. From the teachings of the Buddhas who attained *nirvana*, we know that there are three ways to reach this state:

1. *Rely on upholding precepts.* The *Questions of King Milinda Sutra* says, "If those seeking the Way are settled in upholding precepts and diligently cultivate, they can attain *nirvana* no matter where they dwell, just as people who have eyes can see the sky no matter where they stand. Therefore, *nirvana* relies on upholding precepts." To reach *nirvana*, we should take the precepts as our teacher and diligently cultivate.

2. *Rely on the three Dharma seals.* If we want to achieve Buddhahood, we have to follow the Buddha's teachings. We must contemplate the three Dharma seals: All

conditioned phenomena are impermanent, all phenomena are without an independent self, and *nirvana* is perfect tranquility. The essential point is to understand that all phenomena are empty, and not to have thoughts of attachment or fear regarding phenomena. We must cut off and end all delusions, and be without attachment and clinging. If we accomplish this we will reach the state of *nirvana* in which all phenomena abide in tranquility and attachments are eradicated.

3. *Rely on the threefold training, the four means of embracing, and the six perfections.* To attain the state of *nirvana*, we need to settle the body and mind with the threefold training: morality, meditative concentration, and wisdom. In our practice, we must also use the four means of embracing—giving, kind words, altruism, and empathy—to liberate other sentient beings. Lastly, even in our most trivial activities, we should diligently cultivate the six perfections of giving, morality, patience, diligence, meditative concentration, and *prajna*-wisdom. Each day we should be mindful of doing what is right, and be always transforming our ignorance into awakening.

As one of the three Dharma seals, *nirvana* is the ultimate goal in Buddhism. After the Buddha attained awakening, he saw clearly that all sentient beings generate negative karma because of their ignorance, and as such suffer as they travel the cycle of birth and death. With great compassion, he sought to help sentient beings free themselves from delusion and the suffering of birth and death, eliminate their negative karma, and finally achieve the ultimate state of tranquility. This is why the Buddha taught that "*nirvana* is perfect tranquility."

In this world, human life is fleeting, and only lasts for a few decades of winters and summers, and the human body scarcely grows more than seven feet tall. We face a life with limitations, but if we attain *nirvana*, we will be able to transcend the limitations of time and space. We will overcome the fear of birth and death and the fear of impermanence. Our "life" will then permeate space and time, and we can achieve the state of absolute and complete happiness. Every day we should direct the mind to attaining *nirvana* and finding the true self. We do this by treasuring every second of every minute and diligently cultivating the mind.

Chapter Twelve

THE TRIPLE GEM

Taking refuge in the Triple Gem is the first formal step onto the Buddhist path. Taking refuge signifies that we believe in Buddhism and that we have become disciples of the Triple Gem—the Buddha, the Dharma, and the Sangha. When we take refuge in the Triple Gem, it determines the direction of our faith. When a Buddhist practitioner decides to take refuge in the Triple Gem, it represents a stronger life commitment to learn, practice, and embody the virtues of the Buddha, Dharma, and Sangha.

Gold, silver, diamonds, and pearls are all considered to be treasures in our mundane world. In the world of Buddhism, the Buddha, Dharma, and Sangha are the treasures of our Dharma body and wisdom-life. By making a commitment to the Triple Gem, we reap the benefits of such sublime gems, which ultimately bring us far more meaningful benefits than any material gems could provide.

THE MEANING OF THE TRIPLE GEM

The Triple Gem is the collective term for the Buddha, Dharma, and Sangha.

Buddha is the Sanskrit word for "awakened one." It refers to an awakened being who has awakened to the truth of the universe and has vowed to teach other sentient beings the truth, liberating them with infinite compassion.

Dharma, also a Sanskrit word, has many meanings. The Dharma we are speaking about here means the teachings of a Buddha. Usually, it refers to all of the written teachings contained in the *Tripitaka*, the Buddhist Canon. If sentient beings rely on the Dharma to cultivate, they will realize the truth and attain liberation.

Sangha is a Sanskrit word meaning "community in harmony." It refers to the community of monastics (monks and nuns) who live together in harmony while committing their lives to learning and teaching the Dharma. The sangha is a community that is harmonious in two ways: they have "harmony in principle" and "harmony in practice." Harmony in principle means that all monastics realize the same truth. Harmony in practice means that the monastics' physical, verbal, and mental actions comply with the six points of reverent harmony:

1. Harmony in view through sharing the same understanding, such that there is a common point of view.

2. Moral harmony through sharing the same precepts, such that everyone is subject to the same regulations.

3. Economic harmony through sharing material things and benefits equally

4. Mental harmony through shared happiness, through a common commitment to the Way.

5. Verbal harmony through avoiding disputes by using kindness in one's speech.

6. Physical harmony through living together, such that everyone gets along happily and does not violate one another.

The sangha is a great crucible for cultivating oneself, disciplining one's character, and tempering the mind to sagehood, and as such is a method of self-benefit. The sangha also has the power to transmit the Dharma to help sentient beings liberate themselves, and is this sense does much to benefit others. We can see the importance of the sangha in each of these areas.

To put it simply, the Buddha is like a doctor, the Dharma is like medicine, and the Sangha is like a team of nurses. Each of these three causes are important causes for the liberation of sentient beings. Not one can be lacking. Only when a patient has a good doctor, the proper medicine, and skillful nurses can his illness be cured. This is also true in life, for only by relying on the Buddha, the Dharma, and the Sangha can we be happy, liberated, and free from suffering.

The Buddha, Dharma, and Sangha are called "gems" to show their supreme virtue, for they transcend the value of all worldly treasures. They can relieve our mental suffering and lead us to liberation from the cycle of birth and death.

THE MEANING OF TAKING REFUGE

Taking refuge means that we return to and rely on the Triple Gem, seek protection from the Triple Gem, and attain liberation from suffering through the Triple Gem. Children rely on their parents for protection and safety. Many seniors rely on a cane to walk more steadily. Sailors rely on compasses so they can safely return home. In the dark, people rely on lights so they can see what is in front of them. Likewise, if we have the Triple Gem in our lives, we will have something safe to rely on.

The Triple Gem is also like a compass that can guide us in the great ocean of life towards a safe harbor. If we take refuge in the Triple Gem and learn to appreciate its merit, we can rely on it to cross the sea of suffering and to return to our true home–our Buddha nature. Therefore, taking refuge in the Triple Gem can help us find a safe haven to settle in during this lifetime, and allow us to have a home that we can return to in the future.

THE BENEFITS OF TAKING REFUGE

The Triple Gem is like candlelight on a dark night or the rain that falls to put out the fire of a blazing house. Taking refuge in the Triple Gem not only allows us to attain ultimate liberation, but also gain great benefit in this lifetime. According to the sutras, there are ten benefits of taking refuge:

1. We will become disciples of the Buddha. When we take refuge in the Triple Gem, we accept the greatest sage of all, Sakyamuni Buddha, as our teacher, and we formally become disciples of the Buddha.

2. We will not be reborn in the three lower realms. According to the sutras, when we take refuge in the Buddha, we will not fall into the hell realm. When we take refuge in the Dharma, we will not fall into the animal realm. When we take refuge in the Sangha, we will not fall into the hungry ghost realm. By taking refuge in the Triple Gem, we can escape from the lower realms and will only be reborn in the human or heavenly realms.

3. It will dignify our character. When we don beautiful clothing, our appearance becomes more elegant. After we take refuge in the Triple Gem, our faith deepens and our character becomes more dignified.

4. We will be protected by the Dharma guardians. The Buddha instructed the Dharma guardians and all good deities to protect the disciples of the Triple Gem.

5. We will gain the respect of others. After we take refuge in the Triple Gem, we will receive respect from other people and from heavenly beings.

6. We will accomplish good deeds. By relying on the strength and support of the Triple Gem, we will lessen our negative karma and gain peace and joy. We will then be able to achieve many good deeds in our lives.

7. We will accumulate merit and virtue. According to the sutras, even all the merit and virtue from making offerings cannot compare with the merit of taking refuge. From this,

we can see that the benefits of taking refuge in the Triple Gem are vast and supreme.

8. We will meet good people. Taking refuge in the Triple Gem can help us eliminate our troubles. We will have the opportunity to meet good people and become friends with them. No matter where we go, we will find assistance and make good connections.

9. We will lay the foundation for taking precepts. Only after taking refuge in the Triple Gem are we qualified to take the five precepts and the bodhisattva precepts for laypeople.

10. We can achieve Buddhahood. All who take refuge in the Triple Gem, even if they do not cultivate in this lifetime, will be liberated when Maitreya Bodhisattva comes to this world because they have faith and good karmic conditions.

THE DIFFERENT KINDS OF TRIPLE GEM

There are different classifications for the Triple Gem. The most common classification further divides the Triple Gem into three levels: Initial Triple Gem, Ever-Abiding Triple Gem, and Intrinsic Triple Gem.

1. *Initial Triple Gem.* The Initial Gem of the Buddha refers to Sakyamuni Buddha, who attained awakening under the bodhi tree and manifested thirty-two marks of excellence and eighty notable characteristics. The Initial Gem of the

Dharma refers to the Four Noble Truths, the twelve links of dependent origination, and the three Dharma seals, which the Buddha taught at the Deer Park after he attained awakening. The Initial Gem of the Sangha refers to the Buddha's first five disciples: Kaundinya, Mahanama, Bhadrika, Vaspa, and Asvajit.

2. *Ever-Abiding Triple Gem.* This refers to everything that upholds the Buddha's teachings after his final *nirvana*: all the images of the Buddha, all written sutras, and all monastics that have existed up to the present.

3. *Intrinsic Triple Gem.* At the very moment the Buddha attained awakening under the bodhi tree, he said, "Marvelous, marvelous! All sentient beings have the Tathagata's wisdom and virtue, but they fail to realize it because they cling to deluded thoughts and attachments." Within our intrinsic nature, we already possess the immeasurable merits and virtues of the Triple Gem. All people have Buddha nature; this is the Intrinsic Gem of the Buddha. All people have Dharma nature that is equal and without differentiation; this is the Intrinsic Gem of the Dharma. All people have the nature of the mind that is pure and joyful; this is the Intrinsic Gem of the Sangha.

The act of taking refuge in the Triple Gem is the external force through which we are guided to recognize the true self, affirm the true self, further rely on the true self, actualize the true self, and finally find the Intrinsic Triple Gem within ourselves. Each one of us is like a treasury. By taking refuge, we are discovering the treasures of our mind. When the Buddha was about to enter *parinirvana*, he instructed his disciples to "Take refuge in oneself, take refuge in the Dharma, and do not take refuge in others." This is the true significance of taking refuge in the Intrinsic Triple Gem.

THE PROCEDURE FOR TAKING REFUGE IN THE TRIPLE GEM

Taking refuge in the Triple Gem comes from a deep and heartfelt aspiration to seek the Way. However, many people still go through a refuge ceremony to strengthen and secure their resolve. The sincere act of taking refuge lets our mind connect with the mind of the Buddha. The Buddha's compassion and virtue can improve our bodies and minds. The sincerity in a moment of taking refuge can last a lifetime.

If we have a container that is filled to the top with filthy water, we will not be able to pour in any clean water. Similarly, if our mind is filled with doubt, arrogance, and delusion, we will not be able to accept the pristine Triple Gem. For this reason, the *Sutra of the Great Name* says that all who take refuge must first sincerely repent their previous wrongdoing. Then, with a reverent and pure mind, kneel down and join palms. Before the Buddha, they make the commitment and say:

> I, disciple (*your name*), for the rest of my life, take refuge in the Buddha, the incomparably honored one. I, (*your name*) for the rest of my life, take refuge in the Dharma, honored for being away from defilements. I, (*your name*) for the rest of my life, take refuge in the Sangha, most honored among sentient beings.

(Repeat three times.)

I have taken refuge in the Buddha. I have taken refuge in the Dharma. I have taken refuge in the Sangha.

(Repeat three times.)

Taking refuge in the Triple Gem is our first step towards Buddhahood. This is why we should take refuge under a monastic who is properly qualified. The *Treatise on the Perfection of Great Wisdom,* says:

> When ready to take refuge and prepared to cultivate, go before a monastic. This refuge master will teach one the Dharma of 'good and bad' for distinguishing between right and wrong, to have joy for the good and aversion for the bad, and to open the mind. Then take refuge by saying, "I, (*your name*), for the rest of my life, take refuge in the Buddha, the Dharma, and the Sangha." Repeat this three times. Then say, "I, (*your name*) for the rest of my life, have taken refuge in the Buddha, the Dharma, and the Sangha." Repeat this three times.

These vows are spoken twice during the refuge ceremony. When we say them the first time, we formally accept refuge from the Triple Gem. When we say them the second time, it is at the conclusion of the ceremony.

A typical refuge ceremony has a number of steps. The ceremony begins with paying homage to the Buddhas with three bows. The participants then invite the refuge master to preside over the ceremony. The liturgy begins with singing a short poem called the "Incense Praise" which is used to begin morning and evening chanting, followed by reciting the name of Sakyamuni Buddha three times. Then the participants chant the *Heart Sutra*, a short sutra that summarizes some of the most important Buddhist teachings.

The participants are then asked if they are prepared to take refuge in the Triple Gem. After assenting, the participants repent for any of their previous misdeeds. What follows is the formal taking of the three refuges, with the participants repeating "I take refuge in the Buddha, I take refuge in the Dharma, I take refuge in the Sangha" together. The refuge master then concludes the ceremony by delivering a Dharma talk, often on dedicating the merit of taking refuge. The participants then bow to the refuge master and to the other monastics in attendance. The participants have now officially taken refuge in the Triple Gem.

ANSWERS TO BASIC QUESTIONS
ABOUT TAKING REFUGE

1. Do I need to become a vegetarian after taking refuge?

Taking refuge in the Triple Gem does not require you to become a vegetarian. Taking refuge is the declaration of your commitment to follow the Triple Gem. It has nothing to do with vegetarianism. Those who take refuge do not have to be vegetarians. There is only one requirement when we take refuge: "I follow the Buddha's teachings with unwavering confidence." Some people choose to do this as part of their commitment to purify their mind and actions, but taking refuge in the Triple Gem is not about becoming a vegetarian.

2. After taking refuge, can we participate in other religious practices?

Those who take refuge can still participate in other religious practices, like honoring ancestors or paying respect at non-Buddhist temples. Taking refuge and showing respect are two different things. Taking refuge shows a lifetime commitment, while being respectful is something that happens in a moment. With regard to our ancestors or the deities of other religions, we should be respectful. But it is important to note that these kinds of observances are not the same as the commitment of taking refuge. That being said, after taking refuge we should be committed to seeking the truth, and be wary of superstition.

3. Is taking refuge in the Triple Gem temporary?

Taking refuge in the Triple Gem is not a momentary showing of respect; it is a lifelong commitment. According to the *Yogacara Precepts*, a day without taking refuge is a day without following the precepts. A Buddhist practitioner should renew their commitment to the Triple Gem daily. This very act demonstrates that we, ourselves, do not forget we are Buddhists. By doing this, we deepen our own belief and plant the seeds that can grow into *bodhi*.

4. Does taking refuge in the Triple Gem mean that we worship the monastic who presided over the refuge ceremony?

To take refuge does not mean that we worship the refuge master, simply that we pay homage to the Buddha, learn the Dharma, and respect the Sangha. There are some Buddhists who may call themselves disciples of the Triple Gem, but have only actually taken refuge in one. They may only pay homage to the Buddha, but they do not learn the Dharma or show respect to the Sangha. Some only study the Dharma, but do not pay respect to the Buddha or the Sangha. Others respect the Sangha, but do not pay homage to the Buddha or learn the Dharma. There are even those who only make offerings to the master they took refuge from, or those who treat the Buddha as a god to whom they pray for wealth, blessings, and good fortune. These people are not true Buddhist practitioners. True Buddhist practitioners should not only show respect to all three gems, they should treat all members of the sangha as their teachers as well as study the sutras, learn the Dharma, and be close to Dharma friends. This is the true disciple of the Triple Gem.

Aside from these things, those who take refuge in the Triple Gem must have right view and right thought, believe in cause and effect, and try their best to do good and not harm others. Only in this way can we receive the benefits of the Dharma and of Buddhism.

Chapter Thirteen

THE FIVE PRECEPTS

By taking the precepts, we put our beliefs into practice. After Buddhist practitioners take refuge, they should take a further step by taking the precepts because these precepts are the root of all good things and the basis for all moral conduct. When we follow the precepts, it is like students following the rules of their school or citizens abiding by the law. The only difference is that rules and laws are external forces that regulate our behavior. They are, therefore, considered to be enforced discipline. However, the Buddhist precepts inspire the inner force of self-regulation. This is considered self-discipline. If we do not uphold the precepts, we may make mistakes all the time and bring ourselves misfortune. This is why it is important for Buddhist practitioners to take the precepts.

The five precepts are: refrain from killing, refrain from stealing, refrain from lying, refrain from sexual misconduct, and refrain from consuming intoxicants. It is asked in the *Samyukta Agama*, what it means to fully uphold the lay precepts. The sutra says that laypeople "should stay away from killing, stealing, lying, engaging in sexual misconduct, and consuming intoxicants. Furthermore, they should not wish to commit them. This is called 'fully upholding the lay precepts.'"

Although the precepts in Buddhism are divided into different sets of monastic precepts and lay precepts, the five precepts are the basis of them all. The five precepts are also called the fundamental precepts of Buddhism.

Refrain from Killing

To refrain from killing, broadly speaking, is about not violating or harming the lives of others. Any taking of life is considered killing, from grave offenses such as killing a human being, to less serious cases such as killing ants or mice. However, Buddhism is a religion that emphasizes human beings, so the precept against killing most specifically refers to refraining from killing human beings. In the *Vinaya*, the monastic precepts, killing a human being is one of the most serious offenses, such that any monastic who commits such an offense is immediately expelled from the monastic community. Killing cockroaches, ants and the like is considered an act of wrongdoing, so while it still will carry with it negative karmic effects, it is not on the same level as killing a human being.

Other things like wasting time or squandering material resources can be considered "killing." This is because life is the accumulation of time, so when we waste time, it is like taking a life. Similarly, when we casually destroy material resources, it is also taking away life. This is because material resources belong to all sentient beings, and require the effort of sentient beings to bring about the right conditions for them to come into being.

The main purpose of this precept to refrain from killing is to encourage us to nurture our compassion. The *Mahaparinirvana Sutra* says, "Those who eat meat cut off the seed of great compassion. Whether they are walking, standing, sitting, or lying down, when other sentient beings smell the odor of meat on them, it causes fear and terror." Some Buddhists become vegetarians because they cannot bear to harm chickens, ducks, pigs, lambs, cows, fish, and other animals. However, many also become vegetarians for the sake of cultivating compassion.

Refrain from Stealing

To refrain from stealing is to avoid taking the property and belongings of others. To put it simply, when we take things that do not belong to us without permission, it is stealing. Taking the property of others by force in broad daylight is a more serious violation of the precept. According to the *Vinaya*, if one takes something worth more than five coins (in ancient Magadha currency), it is a violation of the precept.

If we take paper, envelopes, pens, or other supplies from our workplace, or if we borrow things and do not return them, we are engaging in impure conduct. Although it does not break a fundamental precept, we still have to suffer the negative karmic effects and be held responsible for it. Of all the precepts, the hardest to uphold is the precept of not stealing, because we often borrow things for a short period of time and do not ask for permission, or we take others' belongings and keep them as our own.

Refrain from Lying

To lie is to say words that are untrue. This includes being divisive, saying harsh words, and using flattery. Lying can be further divided into three kinds: a great lie, a little lie, and a lie of skillful means.

A "great lie" concerns serious matters, such as when someone who is not awakened claims that they are, or someone who has not realized supernatural powers claims that they have. In addition, gossiping about the faults of sangha members, especially the faults of monastics, is considered a violation of the fundamental precepts.

A "little lie" is committed when you see something but you say you have not, when you do not see something but you say you have seen it, when something is right but you say it is wrong, or when you know something but you claim not to know, and vice versa.

A "lie of skillful means" is more commonly known as a "white lie." An example is when a doctor, considerate of the patient's feelings, withholds information from the patient about the severity of an illness. This kind of lie that is told for the sake of others is a "lie of skillful means."

Refrain from Sexual Misconduct

Sexual misconduct is sexual behavior that violates the law or the rights of others. For example, rape, prostitution, polygamy, pedophilia, sexual slavery, adultery, and other sexual acts that harm and negatively affect our society are all violations of the precept against sexual misconduct. In cases of unrequited love, if we do not commit any acts that harm the person whom we desire, it is not a violation of the precept. However, unrequited love often makes our thoughts unclear, and we become disturbed by our desires and anxieties. This causes us to lose peace of mind. Since the purpose of upholding the precepts is to purify the body and mind, this kind of behavior is contrary to the purpose.

Sexual misconduct is a fuse that ignites chaos in society. For example, the problems of incest and child prostitution are a disgrace to all of civilization. If all people could uphold the precept of refraining from sexual misconduct, these situations would not occur. If all couples resolved to uphold this precept, then families would be in harmony and society would be at peace.

Refrain from Consuming Intoxicants

Not consuming intoxicants refers to not taking substances that dull the senses, causing us to lose self-control and violate the morals of society. For example, alcohol, marijuana, opium, amphetamines, glue, and cocaine are all substances that we should abstain from. However, when the Buddha established this precept, it applied specifically to drinking alcohol.

In the first four precepts, the essential nature of the behaviors that we must abstain from is immoral. The essential nature of drinking alcohol is not itself immoral, but it can cause people to lose self-control and engage in killing, stealing, lying, and sexual misconduct.

According to the *Treatise on the Great Compendium of the Abhidharma*, there was once a layperson who, after getting drunk, stole his neighbor's chicken and broke the precept against stealing. He then killed and cooked the chicken, violating the precept against killing. When his neighbor's wife asked about it, he lied and said that he did not see the chicken, breaking the precept against lying. At this time, he noticed the beauty of the neighbor's wife, so he raped her and violated the precept against sexual misconduct. From this story, we can see that when people drink too much, they may lose their sense of shame, remorse, and self-control. As a result, they may commit any of the four serious crimes of killing, stealing, lying, and sexual misconduct. Therefore, in order to avoid causing harm to others or ourselves, it is best to also uphold this precept and abstain from consuming intoxicants.

THE MEANING OF THE FIVE PRECEPTS

Although the five precepts are different, their fundamental spirit is to not violate others. When we do not violate others but respect them, we will have freedom. For example, to refrain from killing is to not violate the lives of others, to refrain from stealing is to not violate the property of others, to refrain from engaging in sexual misconduct is to not violate the bodies of others, to refrain from lying is to not violate the reputation of others, and to refrain from consuming intoxicants is to not harm our own rational mind and thereby not violate others.

Many people think that the precepts are restrictive, and may wonder why they would want to place such restrictions upon themselves. Actually, upholding the precepts brings freedom and violating the precepts leads to restrictions. If we look carefully at why people have been imprisoned and lose their freedom, we will see that they have violated the five precepts. For example, murder, assault, and disfiguration are all violations of the precept against killing. Corruption, burglary, blackmail, robbery, and kidnapping are all violations of the precept against stealing. Rape, prostitution, abduction, and polygamy are all violations of the precept against sexual misconduct. Slander, breach of contract, and perjury are all violations of the precept against lying. Selling drugs, using drugs, trafficking in drugs, and abusing alcohol are all violations of the precept against consuming intoxicants. People who violate the five precepts will often be imprisoned and lose their freedom.

Therefore, taking the precepts, in many cases, corresponds to abiding by the law. If we can uphold the five precepts and deeply understand them, we will have true freedom. For this reason, the true meaning of upholding the precepts is freedom, not restriction.

Some people think that when we take the precepts we will inevitably break them, but if we do not take the precepts we do not have to worry about breaking them. The truth is, after taking the precepts, even if we break a precept, we are more likely to repent because we have a remorseful heart. Through this act of repentance, we will still have the opportunity to be liberated. When those who do not take the precepts break a precept, they do not know to repent. People who do not feel sorry for harming others cannot improve upon their actions. As a result, they fall into the three lower realms. It is better to take the precepts and repent if we violate them, rather than to not take the precepts and break them. Yet, not taking the precepts does not mean we do not violate them when we do bad things. When we do not take the precepts and we violate them, we still have to bear the negative karmic effects.

THE BENEFITS OF UPHOLDING THE FIVE PRECEPTS

The five precepts are the foundation of all humanity. When we take and uphold the five precepts, we gain endless benefits. According to the *Abhisecana Sutra*, when we uphold the five precepts we will receive the protection of the twenty-five Dharma guardians. The *Moon Lamp Samadhi Sutra* says that those who uphold the precepts with a pure mind will gain ten benefits:

1.   They will have the fulfillment of all wisdom.
2.   They will learn what the Buddha learned.

3. They will become wise, and not be slandered by others.
4. Their *bodhi* mind will not regress.
5. They will be settled in the state of cultivation.
6. They will be free from the cycle of birth and death.
7. They will be able to admire the tranquility of *nirvana.*
8. They will have an undefiled mind.
9. They will attain *samadhi.*
10. They will not be lacking in the Dharma.

If we do not take life but protect it, we will naturally have health and long life. If we do not steal and instead practice giving, we will enjoy wealth and good standing. If we do not engage in sexual misconduct and instead respect the integrity of others, we will have a happy and harmonious family. If we do not lie but praise others, we will gain a good reputation. If we do not drink and stay away from the temptation of drugs, we will naturally have good health and wisdom.

By upholding the five precepts, we can eliminate our suffering, afflictions, and fear in this lifetime, and gain the freedom, peace, harmony, and joy of body and mind. In the future, we can escape from falling into the three lower realms, be reborn in the realms of humans and heavenly beings, and even become a Buddha. Taking and upholding the five precepts is like planting seeds in the field of merit. Even if we do not seek it, we will still have many benefits and immeasurable merit.

UPHOLDING THE FIVE PRECEPTS

When we take and uphold the precepts, we take and uphold them for life. We do not uphold them only for a day. We can take all five precepts at one time, or take only those that we can uphold. The *Treatise on the Perfection of Great Wisdom* says, "There are five precepts. They begin with not killing and end with not consuming intoxicants. If one precept is taken, it is called 'one step.' If two or three precepts are taken, it is known as a 'few steps.' If four precepts are taken, it is known as 'most steps.' If five precepts are taken, it is called 'full steps.' How many steps you wish to take is based on your own conditions."

From this, we see that laypeople can choose which precepts are easier for them to take according to their situation. They can take one, two, three, or four precepts, diligently uphold them, and gradually reach the state where they can uphold all five. In the future, they may also take the eight precepts or the bodhisattva precepts. Through this kind of practice, they will naturally be reborn in the higher realms, be able to reach the supreme states of cultivation, and finally attain Buddhahood.

Chapter Fourteen

THE NOBLE EIGHTFOLD PATH

S uffering is the reality of life. How to attain ultimate liberation from this suffering is the purpose of learning Buddhism. When the Buddha first awakened, he taught eight methods for cultivating the Way towards awakening in order to liberate all sentient beings from affliction and suffering. Together they are called the "Noble Eightfold Path."

By following this Noble Eightfold Path, sentient beings can forever cut off their afflictions, suffering, and the causes of suffering, and attain the state of the sages—*nirvana*. Therefore, this path is called the eightfold path of the sages. The Noble Eightfold Path is like a boat that can carry sentient beings from the shore of ignorance to the other shore of awakening, so it is also known as the boat of eight Dharma methods.

To put it simply, the Noble Eightfold Path is the method for cultivating Buddhahood. It is the way to be free from defilement and suffering. It is the right path of cultivation for Buddhist practitioners. When we follow and practice the Noble Eightfold Path, we can accomplish the ultimate goal of Buddhism. For this reason, as Buddhist practitioners, we should understand the meaning of the Noble Eightfold Path.

THE NOBLE EIGHTFOLD PATH

After he attained awakening, the Buddha taught the Noble Eightfold Path in the first turning of the Dharma wheel. The Noble Eightfold Path is the best representation of Buddhist practice, and for this reason is used to discuss the entire path leading to the cessation of suffering. The Noble Eightfold Path consists of right view, right thought, right speech, right action, right livelihood, right effort, right mindfulness, and right meditative concentration.

Right View

"Right view" is to have the right concepts and right ideas. One concept can change a person's life. The object of learning Buddhism and of cultivating ourselves is to correct mistakes and bad habitual tendencies. This is why having the right views is so important. In the Buddhist sutras, there are many interpretations and explanations of right view. According to the *Lion's Roar of Queen Srimala Sutra*, right views are those views which are not subject to delusion or confusion. The *Flower Adornment Sutra* says that as we develop right view we move farther away from delusion. According to the *Treatise on the Perfection of Great Wisdom*, right view is wisdom. According to the *Introduction to the Stages of Entering the Dharma Realm*, "If one can cultivate without outflows the sixteen aspects of the Four Noble Truths, one will see them clearly; this is called right view."

In summary, right view encompasses observations that lead us away from delusion and wrong views. It is the wisdom that truly comprehends cause and effect. It is the right understanding that results from contemplating phenomena through the three Dharma seals, the Four Noble Truths, and the twelve links of dependent origination. Looking at it from a broader perspective, we can see that all truths of Buddhism are right view.

Right Thought

"Right thought" is also known as right determination, right differentiation, right awareness, or right intention. The *Treatise on the Stages of Yogacara Practitioners* says, "When right view is strengthened, thought without anger and harmfulness arises; this is right thought." Therefore, right thought means to not have thoughts of greed, anger, and ignorance. Instead, it is contemplating and distinguishing the true features of phenomena with wisdom.

The three poisons of greed, anger, and ignorance bind us, and keep us from seeking the Way. At any given moment, these three poisons occupy the mind and pollute the purity of our intrinsic nature. If we wish to leave behind these three poisons, we must be firm in our resolve, we must always contemplate the right Dharma; and we must possess the mind of gentleness, compassion, and purity, free from anger. When our thoughts are in accord with the right Dharma at every moment, we can eliminate the three poisons and grow closer to becoming Buddhas.

Right Speech

"Right speech" is wholesome verbal karma, and also refers to four of the ten wholesome actions: refraining from dishonest speech, divisive speech, harsh speech, and idle chatter. Right speech is to refrain from all careless, slanderous, arrogant, scolding, insulting, mean, flattering, and untrue words. This is why right speech is known as words that are both "right" and "true." When the Buddha taught the Dharma, his words were all true, immutable, and directed towards helping people awaken; this is right speech. There are four kinds of right speech:

1. *Words of truth.* These are words that are true, honest, and not duplicitous.
2. *Words of compassion.* These are words that are kind, soft, and give others confidence.
3. *Words of praise.* These are words that encourage others and bring them joy.
4. *Words of altruism.* These are words that help and benefit others.

Right Action

"Right action" is behavior that is right and in accord with the truth. It is wholesome bodily karma, which includes three of the ten wholesome actions: not killing, not stealing, and not engaging in sexual misconduct. However, following this is just passively not committing unwholesome deeds. The active meaning of right action is to protect life, be compassionate, and give charity.

Furthermore, the *Treatise on the Stages of Yogacara Practitioners* says, "In our lives, or in the pursuit of daily necessities, whether we are walking, standing, sitting, or reclining, if we can perform them with right thought, this is called right action." In other words, having a disciplined lifestyle is right action. For example, proper sleeping habits, diet, exercise, rest, and work habits, will not only improve our health and efficiency, but are also the main elements for a happy family and a peaceful society.

Right Livelihood

"Right livelihood" refers to the right occupation and right way to make a living. According to the *Treatise on the Stages of Yogacara Practitioners,* "Following the Dharma in our pursuit of clothing, food, and other items, or staying away from all the ways of living that give rise to unwholesomeness, is right livelihood." Having a moral profession in life is extremely important because most unwholesomeness comes from doing things that harm others and ourselves. Occupations such as working in a gambling establishment or a brothel, or dealing drugs or arms are not examples of right livelihood because they involve killing, stealing, lying, engaging in sexual misconduct, and selling intoxicants.

Right Effort

"Right effort" is also known as right diligence, right skillful means, and caring for the Dharma. It means that we should move in the direction of truth with courage and diligence. The sutras say, "If laypeople are lazy, they lose the benefits of the mundane world. If monastics are indolent, they lose the Dharma Gem." According to the *Sutra of Mindfulness on the Right Dharma,* indolence is the root of all unwholesome ways; it is the seed of the cycle of birth and death; it gives rise to all affliction and suffering in the world. If we wish to break the cycle of birth and death, we should be diligent and abandon indolence.

Diligence is not disorderly and does not retreat. It strives to do good and strives to not harm. The *Treatise on the Perfection of*

Great Wisdom says that we should take the four right efforts as the goal in our cultivation of diligence. The four right efforts are: to prevent unwholesome states that have not yet arisen, to end unwholesome states that have arisen, to develop wholesome states that have not yet arisen, and to strengthen wholesome states that have arisen.

Right Mindfulness

"Right mindfulness" is also known as true contemplation. It means to have a mind that is pure, aware, and does not give rise to unwholesome thoughts. It is contemplating the right path. The *Sutra of Teachings Bequeathed by the Buddha* says, "If we build a strong foundation of mindfulness, although we are surrounded by thieves of the five desires, we will not be harmed. It is like wearing armor into a battle and fearing nothing." This is why Buddhist practitioners should not pay any attention to gossip, desire, gain or loss, winning or losing, money or fame, and should always maintain right mindfulness. There are four applications of right mindfulness. They are:

1. *Contemplate the impurities of the body.* Attachments and delusions arise because most people are attached to the body, especially to its beauty and health. In fact, our bodies are filled with urine, excrement, mucus, saliva, and other waste products. In fact, the body is where all such waste is produced. The Buddha taught us to contemplate the impurity of the body to eliminate our attachment to the body, so that we can learn to use the body for the sake of cultivation, to attain the Dharma body.

2. *Contemplate the suffering of feelings.* Both the mundane feelings of pain and happiness result in suffering. Life is full of many kinds of suffering, such as birth, aging, sickness, and death. Even when we have a happy feeling, because all phenomena are impermanent, that happy feeling will eventually come to an end. Therefore, we should realize that feelings lead to suffering.

3. *Contemplate the impermanence of the mind.* Our thoughts are changing every minute and every second. Suddenly, they are in heaven; then, they are in hell. Sometimes, they are good; sometimes, they are bad. Sometimes, they arise; sometimes, they recede. For this reason, the Buddha said that we should contemplate the impermanence of the mind.

4. *Contemplate the non-selfhood of phenomena.* The *Diamond Sutra* says, "All conditioned phenomena are like dreams, illusions, bubbles, or shadows, like dew and lightning. One should contemplate them in this way." All phenomena in the world will eventually decay and extinguish; nothing in this world has a substantial existence that is completely separate from anything else. If we know how to contemplate the fact that all phenomena have no substantial existence, "non-self," we can find our intrinsic nature amidst the five desires of wealth, sex, fame, food, and sleep.

By always being mindful of impermanence, suffering, and non-self, we will not be attached to worldly advantages, and can bravely walk towards the Way.

Right Meditative Concentration

"Right meditative concentration" is using *samadhi* to focus the mind and settle the distracted body so we can better cultivate ourselves. True *samadhi* is not merely a matter of sitting in meditation; it is also developing and exploring our inner capacity. Right meditative concentration should bring us good health. It should help us focus on single-mindedness and attain peace. It should clarify the mind and lead us from ignorance to the state of awakening. Ultimately, cultivating right meditative concentration will reveal our Buddha nature to us and allow us to discover our true self.

THE IMPORTANCE OF THE NOBLE EIGHTFOLD PATH

The *Treatise on the Great Compendium of the Abhidharma* says, "Right view gives rise to right thought. Right thought leads to right speech. Right speech leads to right action. Right action initiates right livelihood. Right livelihood initiates right effort. Right effort then gives rise to right mindfulness. Right mindfulness can give rise to right meditative concentration." If people have right view, they will be able to have right thought and determine what is right or wrong, good or bad, and true or false. They will then perform right action of body, speech, and mind, and move in the right direction with right effort. They will also develop right mindfulness and abide in right concentration. We should realize that the Noble Eightfold Path is a unified whole. For any one of them to be fulfilled, it must be accompanied by the other seven elements.

Right view is the first step in the Noble Eightfold Path. Right view is wisdom and the teacher of cultivation. Buddhist practitioners must have right view before they can see the truth of the universe. The *Samyukta Agama* says, "If one has a strong foundation of right view in the mundane world, although they will be reborn a thousand times, they will never fall into the three lower realms." From this, we can see the significance of right view, and understand the importance of the Noble Eightfold Path without having to say a single word.

HOW TO PRACTICE THE NOBLE EIGHTFOLD PATH

The Dharma is not a theory, and we cannot understand it solely from a philosophical point of view. This is especially true of the Noble Eightfold Path, which gives us guidance in our lives. For this reason, we need to practice it each and every day. When we do not change our belief in Buddhism in spite of how difficult it is to practice Buddhism, this is right view. When our every thought is in accordance with the Dharma, this is right thought. When we speak with kind and compassionate words, giving others joy, hope, and confidence, this is right speech. When our actions are in accordance with morality; when we do not harm others just to satisfy our own desires; when we actively come to the aid of those in need of assistance; when we practice giving; when we strive to do good deeds and prevent evil; when we calmly use our wisdom to solve our problems in any kind of situation, these are all ways to practice the Noble Eightfold Path in our daily lives.

Chapter Fifteen

BECOMING A BODHISATTVA

A bodhisattva is a great practitioner who is walking on the path toward Buddhahood by benefiting all sentient beings as well as themselves. The path of the bodhisattva is a long, selfless journey through countless *kalpas* that requires diligent cultivation of patience, compassion, mindfulness, and wisdom. Full of compassion for others, bodhisattvas make the great vow to liberate sentient beings from suffering and help guide them toward awakening.

The word "bodhisattva" is derived from two Sanskrit words: *bodhi* and *sattva*. *Bodhi* means "to awaken" and *sattva* means "sentient being." Therefore, *bodhisattva* means a "sentient being who is seeking awakening." A bodhisattva is a practitioner who is seeking awakening, helps others liberate themselves, cultivates various perfections, and eventually will attain Buddhahood. Bodhisattvas are beings who perfect the practice benefitting both themselves and others in their pursuit of awakening.

LIBERATING SENTIENT BEINGS

All bodhisattvas must make the vow to liberate all sentient beings from suffering. There are two different ways they can fulfill this vow:

1. *First liberate oneself; then liberate others.* Without attaining liberation for oneself, how is it possible to liberate others? When someone is drowning and we do not know how to swim ourselves, how can we save him? Therefore, before helping and liberating others, a bodhisattva must be liberated from the cycle of birth and death and must reach the state without affliction and suffering.

2. *First liberate others; then liberate oneself.* This is precisely the bodhisattva vow. A bodhisattva learns all teachings for sentient beings. If a bodhisattva cultivates the path away from sentient beings, then he can no longer be called a bodhisattva. When bodhisattvas completely liberate all sentient beings, that is when they fulfill the bodhisattva path.

Regardless of the approach we take, when we make a Mahayana vow to seek the Way, helping and liberating sentient beings becomes our primary responsibility. There is a saying for bodhisattvas to describe themselves, "Teaching Dharma is my duty, benefiting sentient beings is my mission."

THE MIND OF A BODHISATTVA

The mind of the bodhisattva has three elements: the aspiration for awakening, great compassion, and skillful means. Master Taixu (1889-1947) said that the aspiration for awakening is the cause, great compassion is the root, and skillful means are the ultimate truth. In Mahayana Buddhism, when practitioners are on the bodhisattva path, they cultivate the mind in this way.

The aspiration for awakening is the mind seeking to attain Buddhahood. Becoming a Buddha requires countless *kalpas* of cultivation. Unless we develop the aspiration for supreme awakening, how can we bear such long-term challenges?

The sutras say that if one more person in the world generates the aspiration for awakening, this creates another seed of awakening. Practicing Buddhism without generating the aspiration for awakening is like tilling the land without sowing seeds. If we do not sow any seeds, how can we have a harvest in the future? The aspiration for awakening leads to making the bodhisattva's four universal vows:

1. Sentient beings are limitless, I vow to liberate them.
2. Afflictions are endless, I vow to eradicate them.
3. Teachings are infinite, I vow to learn them.
4. Buddhahood is supreme, I vow to attain it.

According to the *Flower Adornment Sutra*, "When one loses the aspiration for awakening, even if he cultivates good conduct, it is unwholesome." When bodhisattvas lose the aspiration for awakening, they cannot benefit any sentient beings. Therefore, the aspiration for awakening is the root of all wisdom and the basis for practicing great compassion.

Great compassion is the quality of mind that wishes to liberate sentient beings. When a bodhisattva wishes to come to the aid of sentient beings, they must do so with a mind imbued with great loving-kindness and great compassion. A bodhisattva uses their great loving-kindness to bring others joy, and their great compassion to remove the suffering of others. Bodhisattvas should treat the suffering and happiness of all sentient beings as their own. When they liberate sentient beings, they do not seek anything in return, but instead see helping others as their responsibility. A bodhisattva is one who wishes to shoulder the burden of sentient beings, and hopes to liberate others from suffering rather than seeking peace and happiness for themselves. This is truly great compassion.

Skillful means can be implemented by practicing the four means of embracing. Sentient beings have different capacities to understand the Dharma, so bodhisattvas must wisely apply skillful means to liberate them. Having observed the different capacities of sentient beings, the Buddha taught 84,000 teachings, which all became the Buddha's skillful means. A bodhisattva applies the four means of embracing—giving, kind words, altruism, and empathy— so that sentient beings can be happy.

THE CHARACTERISTICS OF A BODHISATTVA

The bodhisattva's most unique characteristics are compassion and selflessness. Whenever bodhisattvas see sentient beings suffering, great compassion arises from deep within them, and they make the great vow to liberate sentient beings from suffering. Therefore, compassion is the force that moves bodhisattvas to attain Buddhahood by benefitting themselves and others.

The compassion that bodhisattvas have for sentient beings is like the love that parents have for their children. To fulfill their needs, they would be willing to sacrifice their own lives. A bodhisattvas' great loving-kindness and compassion extends to all sentient beings just as the sun shines on every corner of the land. Bodhisattvas use their compassion as a foundation to apply *prajna*-wisdom to liberate sentient beings based on the needs of each of them.

One of the greatest bodhisattvas is Avalokitesvara Bodhisattva, who is known as the bodhisattva of compassion. With his incomparable compassion, he made twelve great vows to liberate all sentient beings. The name of Avalokitesvara Bodhisattva is translated into Chinese as *guanshiyin* (觀世音), "observing the sounds of the world," for at any time and any place, he is able to observe the cries of those seeking assistance and applies his supernatural powers and skillful means to manifest before sentient beings. So long as there are sentient beings who cry out for help, Avalokitesvara Bodhisattva will appear and respond. In accordance with the various needs of sentient beings, he manifests in thirty-two bodily forms wherever he is needed to relieve suffering and distress.

In the Universal Gate chapter of the *Lotus Sutra*, the Buddha explains to Aksayamati Bodhisattva why Avalokitesvara Bodhisattva is known as "observing the sounds of the world":

Aksayamati Bodhisattva said to the Buddha, "World-honored One, how did Avalokitesvara Bodhisattva come to this Saha world? How does he teach the Dharma for the sake of living beings? How does he apply the power of skillful means?"

The Buddha told Aksayamati Bodhisattva, "Good men, if there are living beings in this land who should be liberated by someone in the form of a Buddha, then Avalokitesvara Bodhisattva will manifest in the form of a Buddha and teach the Dharma to them."

"For those who should be liberated by someone in the form of a *pratyekabuddha*, then he will manifest in the form of a *pratyekabuddha* and teach the Dharma to them. For those who should be liberated by someone in the form of a *sravaka*, then he will manifest in the form of a *sravaka* and teach the Dharma to them.

"For those who should be liberated by someone in the form of King Brahma, then he will manifest in the form of King Brahma and teach the Dharma to them. For those who should be liberated by someone in the form of Lord Sakra, then he will manifest in the form of Lord Sakra and teach the Dharma to them. For those who should be liberated by someone in the form of Isvara, then he will manifest in the form of Isvara and teach the Dharma to them.

"For those who should be liberated by someone in the form of the Mahesvara, then he will manifest in the form of the Mahesvara and teach the Dharma to them. For those who should be liberated by someone in the form of a great heavenly general, then he will manifest in the form of a great heavenly general and teach the Dharma to them. For those who should be liberated by someone in the form of Vaisravana, then he will manifest in the form of Vaisravana and teach the Dharma to them.

"For those who should be liberated by someone in the form of a lesser king, then he will manifest in the form of a lesser king and teach the Dharma to them. For those who should be liberated by someone in the form of an elder, then he will manifest in the form of an elder and teach the Dharma to them. For those who should be liberated by someone in the form of a layperson, then he will manifest in the form of a layperson and teach the Dharma to them. For those who should be liberated by someone in the form of a minister, then he will manifest in the form of a minister and teach the Dharma to them. For those who should be liberated by someone in the form of a brahman, then he will manifest in the form of a brahman and teach the Dharma to them.

"For those who should be liberated by someone in the form of a *bhiksu*, a *bhiksuni*, an *upasaka*, or an *upasika*, then he will manifest in the form of a *bhiksu*, a *bhiksuni*, an *upasaka*, or an *upasika* and teach the Dharma to them.

"For those who should be liberated by someone in the form of a woman who is an elder, a layperson, a minister, or a brahman, then he will manifest in the form of a woman and teach the Dharma to them.

"For those who should be liberated by someone in the form of a young boy or young girl, then he will manifest in the form of a young boy or young girl and teach the Dharma to them.

"For those who should be liberated by someone in such forms as a *deva*, a *naga*, a *yaksa*, a *gandharva*, an *asura*, a *garuda*, a *kimnara*, a *mahoraga*, human or non-human being, then he will manifest in all these forms and teach the Dharma to them.

"For those who should be liberated by a vajrapani deity, then he will manifest as a vajrapani deity and teach the Dharma to them.

"Aksayamati, such is the merit that Avalokitesvara Bodhisattva has accomplished, and the various forms in which he wanders the various lands bringing liberation to living beings.

"This is why all of you should single-mindedly make offerings to Avalokitesvara Bodhisattva, for it is the great Avalokitesvara Bodhisattva who can bestow fearlessness in the midst of terror and in dire circumstances. This is why everyone in this Saha world calls him the bestower of fearlessness."

To Mahayana Buddhists, Avalokitesvara Bodhisattva is widely considered to be the very embodiment of the Buddha's compassion. His deep cultivation is characteristic of the bodhisattva's compassion and selflessness.

THE PRACTICE OF THE BODHISATTVA PATH

Buddhism is a religion that emphasizes practice, but it is also a philosophy with ethical characteristics. The Buddhist sutras contain many profound doctrines on truth and the universe, and in this sense it can be considered a philosophy. However, Buddhism places great emphasis on the application of morality and ethics to life, so it can be classified as a religion. In fact, the Buddha himself was regarded as a moral role model. After the Buddha attained awakening, he repeatedly taught that we should, "Do nothing that is unwholesome, do all that is wholesome, and purify the mind" with the hope that all sentient beings could purify themselves through moral conduct.

Practicing the bodhisattva path is just like any other kind of learning; one must go step by step. From the state of an ordinary person who has afflictions to the state of the bodhisattva who has cut off all defilements, there are definite stages of cultivation. In order to progress through these stages and become a sage, a bodhisattva must fulfill the thirty-seven aspects of awakening, the four means of embracing, and the six perfections.

The "thirty-seven aspects of awakening" are the four bases of mindfulness, the four right efforts, the four bases of spiritual power, the five faculties, the five strengths, the seven factors of awakening, and the Noble Eightfold Path. These methods are the resources that can help us cut off unwholesome deeds, develop wholesome conduct, eliminate ignorance, and enter the path of awakening. For these reasons, the practitioners on the bodhisattva path should diligently cultivate these thirty-seven aspects of awakening.

However, the most important teaching for developing the bodhisattva path is that of the six perfections. Called the six *paramita* in Sanskrit, it means "leading to the other shore" or having accomplished the goal of awakening. The six perfections liberate us from delusion and lead us to awakening, liberate us from evil and lead us towards the right path, and liberate us from suffering and grant us happiness. The six perfections liberate all sentient beings from the shore of affliction and ferry them to the other shore of liberation. The six perfections are forms of practice that bodhisattvas must cultivate in order to become Buddhas:

1. *The perfection of giving.* To be generous without any attachment to form is the perfection of giving. All gifts

should be given without any attachment to what is being given, who is giving, or who is receiving the gift. This is the way that a bodhisattva gives.

2.   *The perfection of morality.* This is to respect and not violate sentient beings. Observing the Buddhist precepts, acting in accordance with right Dharma, and practicing the path of benefiting sentient beings is the bodhisattvas' way of upholding the precepts.

3.   *The perfection of patience.* This is the sense of equanimity that allows us to endure what is difficult to endure. To learn all teachings, one should practice patience by being tolerant in the face of persecution, by being accepting amidst adversity, and by contemplating all truths. When one is able to do what is difficult to do and endure what is difficult to endure without retreating in fear, this is the bodhisattvas' way of practicing patience.

4.   *The perfection of diligence.* This means to fearlessly refrain from what is unwholesome and do what is wholesome. Bodhisattvas do not fear obstacles, but diligently develop courage, diligently practice the Dharma, and diligently bring joy and benefit to others. They do not tire of teaching even the most obstinate of sentient beings and apply their efforts ceaselessly.

5.   *The perfection of meditative concentration.* This means to not differentiate with the mind and maintain right mindfulness. Bodhisattvas apply meditative concentration to

settle themselves and others, and to demonstrate right mindfulness to all sentient beings.

6.   *The perfection of prajna-wisdom. Prajna* is the great wisdom that is beyond the duality of emptiness and existence. Bodhisattvas skillfully apply their *prajna*-wisdom to inspire sentient beings to do what is right and good, and gradually liberate them from their suffering.

The six perfections of a bodhisattva are altruistic and profound. A true practitioner practices the six perfections and protects the Dharma, allowing it to spread throughout the universe. Such a person sincerely strives to create a bright future to benefit our communities. When we can generate the same compassion and the same aspiration for awakening as the bodhisattvas, and cultivate the six perfections for our own benefit and the benefit of others, then the Pure Land of Humanistic Buddhism will appear before us.

Chapter Sixteen

HUMANISTIC BUDDHISM

The founder of Buddhism, Sakyamuni Buddha, was born into this world. He cultivated himself in this world, attained awakening in this world, and shared with others the deep truths he realized in this world. The human world was emphasized in everything he did.

Why did the Buddha attain awakening as a human being, and not as a heavenly being, an *asura*, an animal, a ghost, or in hell? Taking this question one step further, why did the Buddha not attain awakening in the distant future or the forgotten past? Why did he choose our world and our time? There can only be one reason: the Buddha wanted the teachings of Buddhism to be relevant to the human world.

The Buddha's life as a human being can serve as inspiration and as a model for spiritual practice in our own lives. We call the teachings of the Buddha "Humanistic Buddhism" to emphasize that they can be integrated into all aspects of our daily lives. Humanistic Buddhism has six characteristics:

1. *Humanity.* The Buddha did not come or go without leaving a trace, nor was he some sort of illusion. The Buddha was a living human being. Just like the rest of us, he had parents, a family, and he lived a life. It was through this human life that he showed his great loving-kindness and compassion, his moral character, and his wisdom.

2. *Emphasis on daily life.* The Buddha taught that we must practice his teachings in our daily lives. He provided guidance on everything, from how to eat, dress, work, and live, to how to walk, stand, sit, and sleep. He gave clear directions on every aspect of life, from how to maintain our relationships with family and friends to how we should conduct ourselves in the social and political arenas.

3. *Altruism.* The Buddha was born into this world to teach, to provide an example, and to bring joy to all beings. He nurtured all beings, for he always had the best interests of others in his mind. In short, his every thought, word, and action arose from a deep care and concern for others.

4. *Joyfulness.* The Buddhist teachings give people joy. Through the limitless compassion of his heart, the Buddha aimed to relieve the suffering of all beings so that they could be happy.

5. *Timeliness.* The Buddha arose in this world for one great matter: to build a special relationship with all of us who live in this world. Although the Buddha lived some 2,500 years ago and has already entered *nirvana*, he left the seed

of liberation for all subsequent generations. Even today, the Buddha's ideals and teachings serve as timely, relevant guides for us all.

6. *Universality.* The entire life of the Buddha can be characterized by the Buddha's spirit of wanting to liberate all beings, without exclusion. The Buddha loved beings of all forms, whether they were animals or humans, male or female, young or old, Buddhist or not Buddhist, he cared for all without distinction.

For some, it is difficult to see how Buddhism is relevant to our modern lives. I can still recall a debate I once heard between the Confucian philosopher Liang Shuming, and the great Buddhist reformer Master Taixu. Master Taixu had invited Liang Shuming to lecture at Hanzang Buddhist Seminary, and he began his lecture writing three words on the blackboard: "now," "here," and "us." Mr. Liang explained, "It is because of these three words that I gave up Buddhism and decided to study Confucianism."

After the lecture, Master Taixu offered his insight. Though Buddhism talks about the ancient past and distant future, it particularly emphasizes the universal welfare of beings in the present moment. And while Buddhist cosmology discusses countless other worlds, it is *this* world which is most important. Buddhism acknowledges many kinds of beings within the ten dharma realms, it reserves the most attention for the human condition.

Buddhism is a religion for people, and human concerns are at its root. Throughout the Buddhist sutras the Buddha emphasized that he too was part of the sangha to emphasize that he was not a god. The *Vimalakirti Sutra* states: "The Buddha realm is found among sentient beings. Apart from sentient beings, there is no Buddha. Apart from the assembly, one cannot find the Way." Huineng, the Sixth Patriarch of the Chan School, said, "The Dharma is within the world, apart from this world there is no awakening. Seeking awakening apart from the world is like looking for a rabbit's horn." To become Buddhas, we must train and cultivate ourselves in the world. There is simply no other way. Now that we have been fortunate enough to be reborn as human beings, we should integrate our practice of Buddhism into our daily lives.

In Buddhism, this human birth is seen as a precious thing that we should not take for granted. In fact, the *Samyukta Agama* draws the following analogy: Imagine there is a blind sea turtle in a vast ocean. Floating on top of the vast ocean is a wooden ring, just big enough for the tortoise to fit his head. If the turtle only comes up for air once every one hundred years, the likelihood that he will poke his head through the hole is greater than the chance of being reborn as a human being. The *Agamas* also say, "The number of beings who lose their human birth are as numerous as the particles of dust on the earth. The comparative number of those who are able to gain a human birth are as scarce as the dirt under a fingernail." This shows how rare and precious human life is.

There are some Buddhists who hear about awakening and attaining Buddhahood and think that Buddhism is not for them. People who think this see Buddhism as a religion that is removed from humanity. They see an isolated Buddhism, a Buddhism removed to the mountains and forests, a self-centered Buddhism, and an individual Buddhism. For them it has lost its human quality. It has reached the point where many who are interested in learning more about Buddhism dare not do so; they hesitate as they peer in and wander about outside. We must redouble our effort and affirm that Buddhism is invested in the liberation of all sentient beings.

In the history of Buddhism, the first 100 to 300 years following the Buddha's final *nirvana* was dominated by "Hinayana Buddhism." The following 600 years saw the rise of "Mahayana Buddhism," while Hinayana Buddhism receded from view. The next 1000 years saw the development of esoteric practice, or "Tantric Buddhism." Humanistic Buddhism is an integration of all Buddhist teachings from the time of the Buddha until the present day— whether they are derived from the Early Buddhism, Mahayana, or Tantric traditions.

In China there are four sacred mountains that have become pilgrimage sites due to their association with the four great bodhisattvas: Avalokitesvara, Manjusri, Samantabhadra, and Ksitigarbha. Of these four bodhisattvas, Avalokitesvara, Manjusri, and Samantabhadra manifest themselves as laypersons. Only Ksitigarbha Bodhisattva manifests himself as a monastic. Why? The life of a monastic emphasizes detachment from and transcendence of the mundane world, while the life of a layperson allows for the optimism and engagement that can realize the goals of Mahayana Buddhism.

Bodhisattvas are not only clay statues to be worshipped in temples. A bodhisattva is an energetic and endearing person who strives to guide all sentient beings to liberation. We can all be bodhisattvas. To fully realize the bodhisattva way of life is the goal of Humanistic Buddhism.

In Buddhism there is the concept of the "Pure Land." The Pure Land is a realm created through the power of a Buddha's vows to ease the suffering of living beings. All people would like to live in a place such as this. Buddhists frequently mention Amitabha

Buddha's Pure Land of Ultimate Bliss in the West, or the Medicine Buddha's Pure Land of Azure Radiance in the East. But there are more Pure Lands than just those in the east or west. Maitreya Bodhisattva, who will become this world's next Buddha, resides in the Tusita Pure Land, and the *Vimalakirti Sutra* mentions the Pure Land of the mind. Pure lands are everywhere.

Humanistic Buddhism seeks to create a Pure Land on earth. Instead of resting our hopes on being reborn in a Pure Land in the future, why don't we work on transforming our world into a Pure Land of peace and bliss? Instead of committing all our energies to some later time, why don't we direct our efforts toward purifying our minds and bodies right here and now in the present moment? Humanistic Buddhism focuses on the world right now, rather than on leaving the world behind, on caring for the living rather than caring for the dead, on benefitting others rather than benefitting oneself, and on liberating all beings rather than self-cultivation.

Whether one practices Theravada or Mahayana Buddhism, Esoteric or Exoteric Buddhism, Buddhism should maintain its emphasis on humanity so that it can remain relevant as times change. Because Humanistic Buddhism attends to the trends of the current age rather than merely following traditions blindly, it is a beacon for the future.

Humanistic Buddhism recognizes that the material and spiritual are equally important in life and therefore calls for a life that provides for both. There is the external world of action, and there is also the internal world of the mind. There is the world ahead of us and the world behind us. If we always insist on charging blindly into what is ahead, we will get hurt. It is important to look back, and look within. Humanistic Buddhism allows for both existence and emptiness, for having many possessions and no possessions, and for community and solitude. By finding the Middle Way in all things, Humanistic Buddhism allows people to achieve a beautiful and wonderful life.

I believe that being willing to serve others, giving others a helping hand, establishing friendly ties with others, and giving others joy are the teachings of the Buddha. Simply put, the goal of Humanistic Buddhism is to make Buddhism relevant in our world, in our lives, and in each of our hearts. Simply close your eyes, and the entire universe is there, within. Even if all people in the world abandon you, your Buddha nature will never leave you.

In today's world, we are all burdened with responsibilities. We all feel stressed from our obligations in our homes, businesses, and families. So how can we live a happy and contented life? If we apply the Buddha's teachings to our everyday lives then the whole universe can be ours, and we can be happy and at peace in all we do. This is the spirit of Humanistic Buddhism.

List of Texts

Venerable Master Hsing Yun extensively quotes the Buddhist sutras throughout his teachings, often sharing short passages from a staggering variety of works. If a reader is moved by a particular passage, the next step of visiting the literature itself can be a difficult one. An alphabetical list of sutras is provided below to assist in this process. The sutras are organized by their titles in English, except in such cases when the Sanskrit name of the text has become commonplace, as in the case of the *Dharmapada*. Each text is also listed with its common Chinese title, both in Chinese characters and pinyin pronunciation.

Abhisecana Sutra
    Guanding Jing   灌頂經

Amitabha Sutra
    Amituo Jing   阿彌陀經

Blue Dragon Commentary on the Diamond Sutra
    Jingang Jing Qinglong Shuchao   金剛經青龍疏抄

Bodhisattva Precepts Sutra
    Pusa Jie Jing   菩薩戒經

Commentary on the Flower Adornment Sutra
    Huayan Da Shuchao   華嚴大疏鈔

Commentary on the Surangama Sutra
Lengyan Jing Shu 楞嚴經疏

Commentary on the Treatise of the Middle Way
Zhong Lun Shu 中論疏

Complete Enlightenment Sutra
Yuanjue Jing 圓覺經

Diamond Sutra
Jingang Jing 金剛經

Eight Realizations of a Bodhisattva Sutra
Ba Daren Jue Jing 八大人覺經

Explanation of the Treatise on the Awakening of Faith in Mahayana
Shi Moheyan Lun 釋摩訶衍論

Flower Adornment Sutra
Huayan Jing 華嚴經

Golden Light Sutra
Jin Guangming Jing 金光明經

Great Stopping and Seeing
Mohe Zhiguan 摩訶止觀

Heart Sutra
Bore Boluomiduo Xin Jing 般若波羅蜜多心經

Introduction to the Stages of Entering the Dharma Realm
  Fajie Cideng Men   法界次第門

Lion's Roar of Queen Srimala Sutra
  Shengman Jing   勝鬘經

Lotus Sutra
  Fahua Jing   法華經

Mahaparinirvana Sutra
  Da Niepan Jing   大涅槃經

Mahaprajnaparamita Sutra
  Bore Jing   般若經

Mahayana Esoteric Adornment Sutra
  Dacheng Miyan Jing   大乘密嚴經

Mahayana Stopping and Seeing Method
  Dacheng Zhiguan Famen   大乘止觀法門

Moon Lamp Samadhi Sutra
  Yuedeng Sanmei Jing   月燈三昧經

Nirvana Sutra of the Northern Tradition
  Beiben Niepan Jing   北本涅槃經

Platform Sutra
  Liuzu Tan Jing   六祖壇經

Questions of King Milinda Sutra
    Milantuo Wang Wen Jing   彌蘭陀王問經

Rain of Treasures Sutra
    Baoyu Jing   寶雨經

Record of Investigations of Mysteries
    Tanxuan Ji   探玄記

Record of Wanling
    Huangbo Duanji Chanshi Wanling Lu   黃檗斷際禪師宛陵錄

Rice Stalk Sutra
    Daogan Jing   稻竿經

Samyukta Agama
    Za Ahan Jing   雜阿含經

Surangama Sutra
    Lengyan Jing   楞嚴經

Sutra of Supreme Meaning
    Liaoyi Jing   了義經

Sutra of Teachings Bequeathed by the Buddha
    Fo Yijiao Jing   佛遺教經

Sutra of the Great Name
    Daming Jing   大名經

Sutra of the Mindfulness on the Right Dharma
  Zhengfa Nianchu Jing   正法念處經

Sutra on the Five Kinds of Suffering
  Wuku Zhangju Jing   五苦章句經

Sutra on the Principles of the Six Perfections
  Dacheng Liqu Liu Boluomiduo Jing   大乘理趣六波羅蜜多經

Treasure Record of the Chan School
  Chanmen Baozang Lu   禪門寶藏錄

Treatise on Abhidharma-skandha-pada
  Fayun Zu Lun   法蘊足論

Treatise on the Awakening of Faith in Mahayana
  Dacheng Qixin Lun   大乘起信論

Treatise on the Four Noble Truths
  Sidi Lun   四諦論

Treatise on the Great Compendium of the Abhidharma
  Dapi Posha Lun   大毗婆娑論

Treatise on the Middle Way
  Zhong Lun   中論

Treatise on the Perfection of Great Wisdom
  Dazhi Du Lun   大智度論

Treatise on the Profound Mahayana
    Dacheng Xuan Lun   大乘玄論

Treatise on the Stages of Yogacara Practitioners
    Yuqieshi Di Lun   瑜伽師地論

Universal Parinirvana Sutra
    Fangdeng Bannihuan Jing   方等般泥洹經

Vimalakirti Sutra
    Weimojie Jing   維摩詰經

Yogacara Precepts
    Yujia Jieben   瑜伽戒本

Glossary

Abhidharma: Sanskrit for "higher doctrine." It is the philosophical treatment of the Buddha's teachings, and the third "basket" of the Buddhist Canon.

Amitabha Buddha: The Buddha of boundless light and boundless life. Amitabha is one of the most popular Buddhas for devotion among Mahayana Buddhists. He presides over the Pure Land of Ultimate Bliss.

animal realm: *See* **six realms of existence.**

anuttara samyak sambodhi: A Sanskrit term meaning complete, unexcelled awakening; an attribute of all Buddhas.

asura realm: *See* **six realms of existence.**

Avalokitesvara Bodhisattva: The bodhisattva of compassion, whose name in Sanskrit means "Observing the sounds of the world." He is known as one of the great bodhisattvas of Mahayana Buddhism, and is very popular throughout China and East Asia.

awakening: The state of awakening to the ultimate truth—freedom from all afflictions and sufferings.

Bodhidharma: First Chinese Patriarch of the Chan School, who is said to have brought Chan from India to China.

bodhisattva: While the term can describe a practitioner anywhere on the path to Buddhahood, it usually refers to a class of beings who stand on the very edge of awakening, but remain in the world to help other beings attain awakening.

bodhisattva precepts: For laypeople, these precepts include a set of 6 major precepts and 28 minor precepts. The six major precepts consist of the five precepts and an additional precept against speaking about the offenses committed by fellow members of the Buddhist community.

Buddha: Sanskrit for "awakened one." Though there are many Buddhas, the term typically refers to Sakyamuni Buddha, the historical Buddha and founder of Buddhism.

Buddhahood: Buddhahood is the attainment and expression that characterizes a Buddha and the ultimate goal of all sentient beings.

Buddha nature: The capacity to become a Buddha that is inherent to all living beings.

causes and conditions: *See* **karma**.

Chan School: One of the schools of Chinese Buddhism, brought to China by Bodhidharma. It emphasizes the cultivation of intrinsic wisdom and teaches that awakening is illuminating the mind and seeing one's intrinsic nature. A major tenet of the Chan School is that the Dharma is wordlessly transmitted from mind to mind.

Consciousness-Only School: One of two primary Mahayana schools that developed in India and asserted that all phenomena originate from consciousness. The school subsequently had major influences on Buddhist thought in China, Japan and Tibet.

cycle of birth and death: This phrase refers to the idea that all beings are continually reborn in and among the **six realms of existence** until they reach **nirvana**.

dependent origination: The Buddhist concept that all phenomena arise due to causes and conditions; thus, no phenomena possesses an independent self-nature. This concept is also referred to as interdependence. The twelve links of dependent origination are ignorance, mental formations, consciousness, name and form, the six sense organs, contact, feeling, craving, clinging, becoming, birth, and aging and death.

Dharma: Sanskrit for "truth." Refers to the Buddha's teachings, as well as the truth of the universe. When capitalized, it denotes both the ultimate truth and the teachings of the Buddha. When the term appears in lowercase, it refers to anything that can be thought of, experienced, or named; this usage is close in meaning to the concept of "phenomena."

Dharma body: One of the three "bodies" of the Buddha. The Dharma body is the aspect of the Buddha that is present throughout all of existence.

emptiness: The concept that everything in the world arises due to dependent origination and has no permanent self or substance. All phenomena are said to be empty of an inherently independent self.

Esoteric School of Buddhism: One of the three major traditions in Buddhism. Among the three major traditions—Theravada, Mahayana, and Esoteric—the Esoteric School developed last in Indian Buddhism.

eight precepts: The eight precepts are a special set of precepts that are usually taken for a short period of time during retreats for lay Buddhists to experience monastic life. They include the five precepts in addition to precepts to refrain from personal adornments like jewelry, watching singing and dancing, and sleeping on fine beds.

five aggregates: The five aggregates make up a human being. They are form, feeling, perception, mental formations, and consciousness.

five precepts: The most fundamental set of Buddhist precepts, or rules of moral conduct, observed by lay and monastic Buddhists alike. They are to refrain from killing, to refrain from stealing, to refrain from sexual misconduct, to refrain from lying, and to refrain from consuming intoxicants.

Four Noble Truths: A fundamental and essential teaching of Buddhism that describes the presence of suffering, the cause of suffering, the cessation of suffering, and the path leading to the cessation of suffering.

four reliances: Four guidelines for Buddhist practitioners to stay on the path. They are to rely on the Dharma, not on an individual teacher; rely on wisdom, not on knowledge; rely on the meaning, not on the words; and rely on ultimate truth, not on relative truth.

four universal vows: Four vows that are said to initiate the seed of awakening in a practitioner if sincerely taken to heart. They are (1) sentient beings are infinite; I vow to liberate them, (2) afflictions are endless; I vow to eradicate them, (3) teachings are infintite; I vow to learn them, (4) Buddhahood is supreme; I vow to attain it.

heavenly realms: Buddhism describes many different heavenly realms in which one can be reborn. Life in the heavenly realms is pleasurable, but impermanent, and one is still subject to the cycle of birth and death. *See* **six realms of existence**.

Huineng: The Sixth Chinese Patriarch of the Chan school of Buddhism and the subject of the *Platform Sutra*, one of the school's most influential texts.

human realm: *See* **six realms of existence**.

hungry ghost: This is considered one mode of rebirth for those that die with large amount of craving. *See* **six realms of existence**.

impermanence: One of the most basic truths taught by the Buddha. It is the concept that all conditioned phenomena will arise, abide, change, and disappear due to causes and conditions.

kalpa: An Indic unit of time measurement. A *kalpa* is an incalculably long period of time spanning the creation and destruction of the universe.

karma: All wholesome and unwholesome actions, speech, and thoughts and their effects. The term literally means "action," though it is much more commonly used to describe the entirety of the Buddhist view of cause and effect. The Buddha stated that the causes, conditions, and rebirth that we encounter in the future are effects of our previous thoughts, words, and deeds. The term "causes and conditions" is used to analyze causal relationships in a Buddhist context. In this form of analysis, a cause denotes the major factor which produces an effect. A condition is a factor whose presence allows for a cause to produce a given effect. In the cause and effect phenomena of the growth of a plant, the seed is the cause, the sprouting of the seed is the effect, and factors such as the soil, sunlight, and water are the necessary conditions.

ksana: Buddhist term describing a moment; the smallest possible unit of time.

Kumarajiva (344-413): Sino-Indian Buddhist monk and a prolific sutra translator. Many of his sutra translations are still commonly chanted in the Buddhist liturgy today.

lotus position: Commonly suggested seated meditation position for those with enough flexibility to do it, which provides ideal stability to sit for long periods of time. It is done by crossing the legs with each foot sitting on top of the opposite thigh. This is also the position in which nearly every seated Buddha figure is portrayed.

lower realms of existence: *See* **six realms of existence**.

Mahakasyapa: One of the ten great disciples of the Buddha. He is known as foremost in ascetic practices, and is considered the First Indian Patriarch of the Chan School of Buddhism.

mani pearl: An orb said to represent the greatness, virtue, and power of a Buddha.

mantra: A sound or a particular group of syllables or words used as a concentration device or incantation formula, sometimes said to provide some sort of protection or power.

Mara: A malevolent being that embodies desire and is an adversary of the Buddha. The name is also used to refer to mental qualities that impede spiritual progress.

merit: Blessings that occur because of wholesome deeds.

Middle Way. The path between the extremes of hedonism and extreme asceticism taught by the Buddha.

Nagarjuna: Born in Southern India in the second or third century. He is the founder of the Madhyamaka School and the author of many commentaries and treatises. His famous works include *Treatise on the Perfection of Great Wisdom*, *Treatise on the Middle Way*, the *Merits of Right Deeds Sutra*, and many more. Therefore, he was given the title "Master of a Thousand Treatises." He is one of Buddhism's most influential philosophers.

nirvana: A state of perfect tranquility that is the ultimate goal of Buddhist practice. It refers to the absolute extinction of all afflictions and desires; it is the state of liberation beyond birth and death.

no-mind: An expression which refers to the mind which is empty of discrimination and transcends the duality of existence and non-existence.

non-self: (*Skt. anatman*) A basic concept in Buddhism that says that all phenomena and beings in the world have no real, permanent, and substantial self. Everything arises, abides, changes, and extinguishes based on dependent origination.

parinirvana: Final *nirvana*. This phrase often refers to the physical death of the Buddha, when all his ties to karma were completely severed.

pratyekabuddha: One who attains awakening on his or her own, without having heard the teachings of a Buddha.

precepts: *See* **five precepts** or **eight precepts**.

prajna: Sanskrit for "wisdom." Typically referring to a transcendent variety of wisdom that comes from seeing the true nature of reality. *Prajna* wisdom is considered the highest form of wisdom.

Pure Land: A transcendent realm created through the power of a Buddha's vow to help ease the suffering of living beings, should they choose to be reborn there.

rebirth: *See* **cycle of birth and death**.

Sakyamuni Buddha: Siddartha Gautama, the historical Buddha and founder of the religion known today as Buddhism. The name "Sakyamuni" means "sage of the Sakyans," which was the name of his clan.

six perfections: Six qualities that bodhisattvas develop on their way to Buddhahood: giving, morality, patience, diligence, meditative concentration, and *prajna*-wisdom.

six realms of existence: Used to describe the basic Buddhist cosmological scheme. The "six realms of existence" refers to possible destinations of rebirth, and includes heaven, the *asura* realm, the human realm, the animal realm, the realm of hungry ghosts, and hell. The six realms also indicate where we reside and all the modes of existence in which some form of suffering is endured due to greed, anger, hatred, and ignorance. When sentient beings die, they are reborn into one of the six realms of existence. The cycle continues as a result of one's karmic actions. Outside of the six realms, exist four additional realms within which beings have transcended suffering: that of the *sravaka, pratekyabuddha,* bodhisattva, and Buddha. Taken together with the six realms previously mentioned they are called the ten dharma realms.

six sense objects: The six senses of human beings are sight, sound, smell, taste, touch, and *dharmas.*

sravaka: Literally "one who has heard." A *sravaka* is one who has been liberated from the cycle of birth and death after listening to the Buddha's teachings, but does not seek to become a Buddha.

sudden enlightenment: An abrupt, immediate realization of enlightenment, often due to a skillful teaching by a master. This was a common technique expounded by the Chan School.

sutra: A Sanskrit word used to describe a variety of religious and non-religious writings, but most commonly used in a Buddhist context to refer to the recorded discourses of the Buddha.

Tathagata: One of the ten epithets of a Buddha, literally translated as "Thus Come One," meaning the one who has attained full realization of "suchness," true essence, or actuality, i.e., the one dwelling in the absolute, beyond all transitory phenomena, so that he can freely come and go anywhere.

ten dharma realms: *See* **six realms of existence.**

three Dharma seals: Three statements of truth in Buddhism which are universally applicable to all phenomena: (1) All conditioned phenomena are impermanent, (2) all phenomena are without an independent self, and (3) *nirvana* is perfect tranquility.

three poisons: Seen as the root causes of all suffering: greed, anger, and ignorance.

Tripitaka: The canon of Buddhist scriptures known as "Three Baskets." It is divided into three categories: the sutras (teachings of the Buddha), the vinaya (precepts and rules), and the abhidharma (commentaries on the Buddha's teachings).

Triple Gem: The Buddha, the Dharma, and Sangha. Referred to as "gems" to indicate their great value, also called the Triple Jewel, or the Three Jewels. The Buddha is the fully awakened one; the Dharma is the teachings imparted by the Buddha; and the Sangha indicates the community of monastics.

Tiantai School of Buddhsim: One of the eight major schools of Chinese Buddhism. The Tiantai School was founded on the *Lotus Sutra* and emphasized balancing practice and study.

About the Author

Venerable Master Hsing Yun is a Chinese Buddhist monk, author, philanthropist, and founder of the Fo Guang Shan monastic order, which has branches throughout Asia, Europe, Africa, Australia, and the Americas. Ordained at the age of twelve in Jiangsu Province, China, Hsing Yun has spent over seventy years as a Buddhist monk promoting what he calls "Humanistic Buddhism"—Buddhism that meets the needs of people and is integrated into all aspects of daily life.

In 1949, Hsing Yun went to Taiwan and began to nurture the burgeoning Buddhist culture on the island. Early on in his monastic career, he was involved in promoting Buddhism through the written word. He has served as an editor and contributor for many Buddhist magazines and periodicals, authoring the daily columns "Between Ignorance and Enlightenment," "Dharma Words," and "Hsing Yun's Chan Talk." In 1957, he started his own Buddhist magazine, *Awakening the World*, and in 2000, the first daily Buddhist newspaper, the *Merit Times*.

Hsing Yun has authored more than one hundred books on how to bring happiness, peace, compassion and wisdom into daily life. These works include *For All Living Beings, Humanistic Buddhism: A Blueprint for Life,* and *Chan Heart, Chan Art*. He also edited and published the *Fo Guang Encyclopedia*, the most authoritative Buddhist reference work in the Chinese language. His contributions have reached as far as sponsoring Buddhist music and art to creating Buddhist programming for television, radio, and the stage.

Today Master Hsing Yun continues to travel around the world teaching the Dharma. In 2010 he delivered around 120 lectures and gave nearly 30 interviews for television and radio. He continues to write a daily column for the *Merit Times*, as well as to produce one-stroke calligraphy paintings. He is also the acting president of Buddha's Light International Association (BLIA), the worldwide lay Buddhist service organization.

About Buddha's Light Publishing

Buddha's Light Publishing offers quality translations of classical Buddhist texts as well as works by contemporary Buddhist teachers and scholars. We embrace Humanistic Buddhism, and promote Buddhist writing which is accessible, community-oriented, and relevant to daily life.

Founded in 1996 by Venerable Master Hsing Yun as the Fo Guang Shan International Translation Center, Buddha's Light Publishing seeks to continue Master Hsing Yun's goal of promoting the Buddha's teachings by fostering writing, art, and culture. Learn more by visiting www.blpusa.com.